THE MAFIA HIT MAN'S DAUGHTER

LINDA SCARPA
WITH LINDA ROSENCRANCE

Foreword by Marc Songini

PINNACLE BOOKS
Kensington Publishing Corp.
http://www.kensingtonbooks.com

Some names have been changed to protect the privacy of individuals connected to this story.

PINNACLE BOOKS are published by

Kensington Publishing Corp.
119 West 40th Street
New York, NY 10018

All Kensington Titles, Imprints, and Distributed Lines are available at special quantity discounts for bulk purchases for sales promotions, premiums, fund-raising, and educational or institutional use. Special book excerpts or customized printings can also be created to fit specific needs. For details, write or phone the office of the Kensington special sales manager: Kensington Publishing Corp., 119 West 40th Street, New York, NY 10018, attn: Special Sales Department, Phone: 1-800-221-2647.

Pinnacle and the P logo Reg. U.S. Pat. & TM Off.

ISBN-13: 978-0-7860-3870-1
ISBN-10: 0-7860-3870-5
First Kensington Mass Market Edition: January 2016

eISBN-13: 978-0-7860-3871-8
eISBN-10: 0-7860-3871-3
First Kensington Electronic Edition: January 2016

10 9 8 7 6 5 4 3 2 1

Printed in the United States of America

*This book is dedicated to my brother Joey.
I never got to say good-bye, and if given the
chance, I don't think that I could have.—LS*

*For Adam and Cheryl, George and Eva,
and my friend, Kevin Schultz, in Seattle.—LR*

FOREWORD

Behind even the worst Mafia Capo or hitman are a loving and longsuffering wife and family that enable his violent, parasitic, and dangerous lifestyle. Young, pretty, and innocent Linda Scarpa found this out the slow hard way.

Greg Scarpa, the man she called lovingly "Daddy," was justly renowned on the New York streets as the "Grim Reaper." As Colombo family high lord executioner, he was possibly the most violent and ruthless killer inducted into the American Mafia.

In her memoir, *The Mafia Hit Man's Daughter*, Linda Scarpa's clear and machine gun-direct prose depict her journey from an innocent, sweet daddy's girl to a helpless and hapless victim of abuse and violence. One by one, her beloved friends and family members vanish into jail or the grave because of the Mafia's perverse codes. Here is another contribution to the drama of the decline of the once mighty Five Families of New York. In the end, despite the easy money and good times, Scarpa demonstrates Mafia daughters and wives end up just as lonely, loveless, depressed and broke as the rest of us—but with the threat of sudden death or maiming a permanent companion on the entire road there. The "Life," as she says, is full of "misery, death and nightmares."

Greg Scarpa claimed he stopped counting his hits after number 50. Scarpa should have included as victims his wives, daughter and other family members—they all suffered at his hands.

Marc Songini

CHAPTER 1

ONCE AROUND
THE PARK

I was in my sophomore year at Bishop Ford Central Catholic High School in the Park Slope section of Brooklyn, New York. I wasn't quite sixteen yet, but I was growing up a little bit too fast. Always dolled up and looking older than I was.

My younger brother, Joey, was a freshman. Every day we were taken back and forth to school by a car service. The same driver—a Spanish guy—picked us up every morning around 7:45. His name was Jose Guzman.

One day Joey was sick and I went to school alone. That day I was wearing a button-up blouse, mini-skirt, leggings and high heels—always with the high heels.

When the driver came to pick me up, I opened the door to hop in the backseat like we always did. But the guy said, "Oh, you're alone. Why don't you sit in the front with me?" I figured okay because I was used to him, so I sat in the front.

As he started to drive away from the house—we were living on Avenue J at the time—he said, "You know, if you don't mind, I have to pick somebody else up before I take you to school." So I said sure, as long as I got to school on time. I was a kid; I didn't know what was going on. He said, "Oh, yeah. No problem. It's just going to take a couple of minutes."

He took a left onto Coney Island Avenue and drove for about ten minutes. He got to a traffic circle and then headed into Prospect Park. I had no idea what was happening.

"Who do you have to pick up? You're going in the park?"

"Yeah, don't worry about it. I have to pick somebody up."

He drove to a very secluded area in the park and stopped the car. Obviously, I knew something wasn't right. He started telling me that I was so beautiful, and that he couldn't take his eyes off me, and how much he was attracted to me—all this sexual stuff. I was so scared. I had to figure a way out of there.

"I really have to go to school."

"Yeah, well, you're not going to school right now."

"Listen, if you don't take me to school now, the school's going to call my house. My parents are going to know that I'm not at school."

"Oh, don't worry about that—I'll get you to go school, eventually."

Then he grabbed my hand, and—I'll never forget this—he put it up to his mouth. And he licked the crease between my index finger and my middle finger as if they were my legs.

"That's what I'm going to do to you, baby."

And then as he was doing that, he ripped my shirt open. Then this big guy started coming over toward my side of the car, and I was in a panic.

"Oh, my God. You can't do this. I have to go to school."

I was a kid and I wasn't thinking clearly at first about how to handle what was happening. When he was about to do whatever he was going to do to me, I said, "Listen, my parents are going to know. The school's going to call them. It doesn't have to be like this."

He was kissing my neck. So I tilted my head back and I started to let him do it. Then he started grabbing me and pulling at me. Really getting into it, like he was ready to attack me. God only knew what he was going to do after that. All that was going through my head was that I was going to get killed—raped and then killed.

"It doesn't have to be like this. I'll meet you after school. Pick me up after school."

Then he just stopped.

"What are you going to tell your parents?"

"I'll tell them I'm going over to my friend's house. We'll plan this. You could pick me up every day after school and we'll go somewhere. I'll make up something to tell my parents."

I did everything I could to make him think I was into it as much as he was, so I could get myself out of there.

"Wow. Okay, that's great."

I couldn't believe it. He actually thought that I was okay with it. So he tried to kiss me and touch me. My heart was racing and my stomach was churning. I just wanted to vomit. My whole body was trembling and I could feel the sweat trickling down my back.

"Calm down, everything is going to be okay. We'll have a great time. I'll pick you up after school. Just don't tell anybody. Be sure you don't tell anybody that I took you here."

"No, of course not. I'm not going to tell anybody. I can't wait for you to pick me up. We're going to have a good time. Just get me to school before they notice I'm gone because if I miss my first period, they'll call the house."

"Okay, okay, I'll get you to school. I'll be there— what time do you want me to pick you up?"

"Pick me up at two-thirty."

"Okay, okay."

He drove out of the park. On the way to school, I kept thinking that I got myself out of that—somehow I got myself out of it. He really believed me.

When he dropped me off at my school, he said, "Okay, two-thirty. I'll meet you here."

"Okay, I'll be here at two-thirty."

The minute I got inside the building, I ran to the bathroom. I tried to fixed my blouse and look presentable but I was shaking so bad, I was making it worse. So I just gave up. Then I ran to the pay phone down the hall to call my mother, Linda, who was known as "Big Linda." Everybody called me "Little Linda."

"Mom, pick me up. Now."

"What happened?"

"Pick me up. Now."

"Well, what happened?"

The words stuck in my throat.

"Please, just pick me up. Just pick me up. I'll tell you when you get here."

Then I went back and waited for a while in the bathroom until I figured she'd be outside. I never went into any classrooms.

She got there really fast, even though the school was in the Prospect Park area. I jumped in the car. My face was flushed. My blouse was all untucked; my skirt was wrinkled. I was a mess. As soon as my mother saw me, she knew something bad had happened.

"The guy who drove me to school took me to the park and he tried to have sex with me. He tried to rape me."

She flipped out. Went totally crazy. Crying. Screaming at the top of her lungs in the car. Pounding on the steering wheel.

"What? That motherfucker. That motherfucker!"

Yelling. Totally insane. It was the ride home from hell. All I wanted to do was get to the house. The minute she got in the house, she called my father. He told her not to leave the house.

"Fuck you," my mother told him.

She was crazy. She didn't care what anybody said. She ran into the kitchen and grabbed a huge butcher knife. She raced back out to the car and went to the office of the car service. She told the dispatcher there who she was and asked for the address of the guy who took me to school that day. He told her that he didn't

have his address. He said he didn't even know his
name.

My mother pulled out the knife and put it to the
guy's throat. She told him again she wanted the
driver's name and address. The next thing she knew,
my father and a couple members of his crew showed
up. They beat the shit out of the dispatcher until he
gave up the driver's information.

When my mother got home, she told me everything was going to be okay. He was never going to
come near me again. She said she was going to take
me to school from then on.

I went nuts. I started screaming.

"I'm not going to school. I don't want to go to
school. He's going to come after me."

"Nobody's going to come after you—relax."

Just then my father came home with his crew. He
got all emotional—he was an emotional guy, especially when it came to me.

"Oh, my God. What did he do to you? I want to
know what he did to you."

I told him exactly what had happened.

"He's fuckin' dead. This guy is dead."

I was in total shock. I wasn't thinking about what
he was saying. I just wanted to be safe in my house.
Before I knew it, my father and his crew left. When
they came home, my father told me they went after
him and gave him a beating.

But for the next few days, what Guzman had done
to me—and what he could have done—was weigh-
ing on my father's mind. And he wasn't satisfied
with just giving Guzman a beating. He was also
afraid that Guzman would retaliate and come after

me. Who knows what he would have done to me? Especially since I had told him I would never tell anybody about it.

So my father and his crew went back to Guzman's house. They rang the bell. When he opened the door and saw them, he ran. But he didn't get too far. They shot him in the head.

After they killed him, they came back to the house. My father said, "Listen, this guy is an animal. He got what he deserved. He'll never be able to touch you or anybody else."

He tried to rationalize murdering Guzman by telling me that I would have been dead or raped and in a hospital somewhere if I hadn't been able to get myself away from him.

"And God knows if he's done this to other people."

By telling me that I had actually saved other girls from being raped, my father was trying to make me feel better about the fact that they killed this guy. I was just sitting there looking at my father and listening. I was in total shock. Finally, as horrifying as it was, I began to understand.

"Oh, my God. He's dead. The guy is dead. You killed him? Dad, really, you killed him?"

"Yeah, he's dead. You'll never have to worry about him again."

I felt so bad. I was just a kid.

"Dad, did you have to kill him? Did you have to kill him?"

"Linda, if I didn't do this, who knows if he would've tried to hurt you again? Or, if he would've tried to hurt somebody else. We don't know if he's done this before."

It was crazy. He was trying to rationalize to a kid why he had to kill the guy. I didn't want to believe it.

But the next day I read about Guzman's murder in the newspaper and I knew it was true. The article said he had a lot of money on him when he was murdered. When my father read that, he said, "I wish I had known he had all that money on him. I would have made them take the money after they shot him."

I ripped the article out and kept it in my wallet. Every once in a while I'd take it out and look at it. He had kids and I felt so bad and guilty about him getting killed. But what was I supposed to do, not say anything?

Who knew why he tried to rape me? I could only think he didn't know who my father was.

CHAPTER 2

GREGORY SCARPA SR., LOVING FAMILY MAN

My mother met my father in a bar in her Brooklyn neighborhood in the early 1960s when she was just a teenager. She was seventeen when she became his mistress. He was in his mid-thirties—and married. He told her he was involved with the Colombo crime family. Unlike other Mob guys, my father told her about everything—the burglaries, the numbers racket, the murders—everything.

I'll let her tell you about it.

When I grew up in Brooklyn, I lived in an area where there were mostly made guys. All the guys used to go to my grandmother's house—to the back room—and have crap games and take numbers. In fact, my grandmother took the numbers. She used to pick up the numbers at church at six in the morning and give them to me, and I used to hand them to all the guys in the back room.

I was probably eleven or twelve when I was first exposed to these guys. They were all really nice. If you needed anything, they were always there for you. If they were winning in the crap games or something, they would give you money. They were very generous. I knew they were gangsters, but with us, the people they knew, they were just great. I grew up with them, and I thought they were great.

I started dating a made guy from the Gambino crime family, Larry Pistone. We'd go to the Copacabana in Manhattan—I was at the Copa almost every night—and the Latin Quarter club. We were always out for dinner. He gave me money for clothes, to get my hair done, whatever I wanted. But I also saw a bad side of him. One time we had to pick up money from someone. Larry knocked on the door; the guy's wife answered. Then I saw him pull the guy out and hit him. That was the first time I really saw a bad side of one of those guys.

I had been dating Larry for about a year and a half. One night when I wasn't going out with Larry, a friend of mine called and asked if I wanted to go to this new bar that had just opened at Seventy-Second Street and Thirteenth Avenue in Brooklyn called the Flamingo Lounge.

We went to the club and some of my father's friends were there. We were having a few drinks at the bar. At one point I turned around, and in walked this very handsome man with a big smile on his face. I didn't know at the time but he was Greg Scarpa.

He came over to the bar, took his jacket off—he

was dressed real sharp—and looked at me. He knew one of my father's friends and asked him to introduce us. I thought, *Wow,* but I still didn't realize that he was a gangster yet. I just knew he was really unique.

After we were introduced, he stood next to me, bought me a drink and started talking to me.

"You know, you have the most beautiful black eyes. They're like olives, black olives. Do you work?"

I told him I had just gotten a job on Wall Street.

"Well, you know what I would love to do, Linda? I would love to air-condition that train that you ride on, and just do everything for you."

"Oh, Greg, that's a new one."

I had never heard that line before. That night, I knew there was something there. I could see it in him, too, because he came right over to be introduced to me. I was charmed by him, but I didn't even know he was a gangster. The smile on his face—it was just a beautiful smile.

As we were talking, I said to him, "Come on. Do you dance?"

"Of course, I dance."

"Well, come on, let's dance."

So he took my hand and led me onto the dance floor. When it was time for me to leave, he asked for my number. But I was dating Larry at the time, so I told Greg I needed time to break up with Larry.

"Well, you know what, Greg? I'll call you."

"Oh, you want to call me? You'll wait a week or two."

"No. I promise you, I will call you."

So he gave me his number. A few days went by and I still hadn't called him. But I did go out with

Larry and we continued going to the Copacabana. We were ready to leave one night when Larry's wife pulled up in front of the Copa. I didn't want any trouble so I got in a cab and went to the Flamingo Lounge, where Greg was.

I told Greg what had just happened and he wanted to know what I was doing with Larry. As we were talking, I heard a horn beeping outside the club. We were sitting by the window at the bar and I looked out and saw Larry. He knew I used to go to the Flamingo.

Greg and I went outside. Larry said, "Linda, get in the car." I told him no.

"She's coming with me," Greg said. Now I still didn't realize that Greg was a gangster, but I knew Larry was a gangster.

"Well, Greg, maybe I should go."

"No, get in the car," Greg said. His car was parked right in front.

I got in Greg's car and Larry pulled right up next to us.

"Linda, get in the car, come on."

I told Greg I should probably just go with Larry. Then, all of a sudden, I see Greg bending down under his seat.

"No, don't do that, Greg. He's a gangster."

Meanwhile, so was Greg.

"Let me just go with him. I'll talk to him and I'll tell him that it's over."

I got out of Greg's car, and I went with Larry. I told Larry that I didn't want to see him anymore, especially after what had happened with his wife. I said I didn't want to be bothered. Then I told him to take me home. He was apologizing like crazy, but I told him just to take me home.

A day or two later I went to the Flamingo and Greg was in the bar. He told me what had been happening.

"I have a sit-down."

"What do you mean you have a 'sit-down'?"

He told me it was a sit-down with Joe Colombo, Larry Pistone and somebody from the Gambino family that Larry was with. It was over me. At that point I knew Greg was a gangster in the Colombo family. So he went to this sit-down, and they were arguing back and forth.

Joe Colombo finally asked, "What does Linda want?"

Greg said, "She wants to be with me, and I want to be with her."

Greg came out the winner. Larry wasn't supposed to go near me anymore. I was Greg's, and that was it. And that was how it ended with Larry, and I started seeing Greg.

After that I was with Greg every day, and every night. He used to send beautiful fruit baskets to my house every day. I lived with my father, and my father loved it. But he didn't know I was seeing a gangster. He wanted to know who was sending the fruit baskets. I told him it was this really nice guy named George I had just met.

That went on for a week or two. And then, all of a sudden, Greg started sending flowers instead. My father wanted to know why he was sending flowers.

He told me to tell him to send the fruit baskets again.

Greg bought me a car. He bought me a little dog, a French poodle. I told Greg I was going to give the dog to my father to keep him company. He said whatever I wanted to do was fine. It was all about me—whatever made me happy is what he did.

As we got closer, he told me all about himself and his family. He was born in Brooklyn in 1928. He was the second of five kids born to Italian immigrants. He had one brother, Sal, and three sisters, Marie, Vincenza and Theresa, who wasn't well. His mother, Mary, used to take care of her.

At one point Theresa was in the hospital. One day while she was there, the family brought her food. They left her alone for a few minutes while she was eating. She choked on the food and died.

When Greg was really young, about seven, he had to work with his father, who used to deliver coal. Greg hated it and always wanted to live a better life—the same type of life the local gangsters were living.

When we were dating, Greg used to take me to his mother's house in Brooklyn for dinner. She made the greatest homemade pasta. When I had Linda, she knitted beautiful outfits for her.

Greg was a family man. Everything was about his family. He just adored his family and the people close to him, and nobody could talk bad about them. Greg and I spent a lot of time with his sister Marie and her husband, Tony. When we bought our condo in Florida some years later, they bought one right next door to us. We were really close to Marie and her husband.

Greg and Sal used to always butt heads. He loved Sal, but Sal was a thickhead and never listened to Greg. When Sal got made, he wasn't in the Colombo family, but he became part of that family later on.

Sal got involved with the Mob first. By the time Greg was about seventeen, he was pretty street-smart. He caught the eye of local mobster Charlie LoCicero of the Profaci crime family, who recruited him into the life.

Greg told me about the ceremony when he was made in 1950. First, he said, he had to be accepted for membership by all the guys in the family. Then he was called to a meeting with the boss, the underboss, the consigliere, all of the captains and the member who proposed him for membership.

The boss then asked him if he was willing to kill and obey any orders given to him by his bosses. When Greg said yes, the boss who was running the ceremony asked if he was left-handed or right-handed. When he said he was right-handed, the boss pricked the trigger finger of that hand. A few drops of Greg's blood spilled onto a card bearing the image of a saint.

The card was set on fire and, Greg said, he had to pass the card quickly from hand to hand so he wouldn't get burned. While he was moving the card from one hand to the other, he took the oath of loyalty in Italian to the Mafia family: "With this oath I swear that if I ever violate this oath, may I burn as this paper." During the ceremony Greg was specifically asked if he would participate in a killing. If he had said no, he wouldn't have been made.

When my father met Greg, I introduced him as

"George," and Greg went right along with it. My father loved him. A couple days after they met, my father went to the club to play cards. Sonny, one of the guys at the club, told him I was going out with a big gangster named Greg Scarpa. He said I couldn't be going out with Greg Scarpa because I was seeing some man named George.

When my father got home, he had some questions for me.

"Linda, this guy, Sonny, just told me that you're going out with Greg Scarpa."

"Well, yeah, Dad. But you've met him, and he's really a nice guy."

"Greg Scarpa?" My father was in shock because Greg was a really big gangster.

I told Greg what had happened—that one of the guys from the club—a guy he knew, too—told my father about us. And that guy got a few smacks for opening his mouth.

On the street I knew everyone feared Greg. To me, I couldn't understand it because he was a sweetheart. He did everything for me. People were afraid to go into the Flamingo Lounge because they were afraid to meet up with him. But I didn't know him like that—to me, he was the best. He was always taking me to beautiful restaurants for dinner and drinks.

He had my birthday that first year at the Copacabana. I walked in with him and there was Joe Colombo and a whole bunch of goodfellas sitting at the table. I was getting all these beautiful gifts. It was great to have the respect. People who had never talked to me before would pass me on the street and ask how I was doing. When I was at the Flamingo,

I'd order Chinese food from a nearby Chinese restaurant. When they delivered it, the guy always told me I didn't have to pay. So I ordered Chinese food almost every night.

Greg and I spent as much time as we could together. He used to pick me up in the daytime, and we'd go to the park and walk around. Then we'd sit in the car just making out. He fell in love right away, and I could tell. He was a happy person, caring, giving to those he loved. But if you did him wrong, he would kill you.

If you hurt his family in any way or disrespected them, Greg wasn't the type of person who believed in just giving you a beating, because then you could go to the cops and talk. So either you didn't say anything or Greg would kill you. That's what he did. It was just part of the lifestyle—a lifestyle that he didn't hide from me.

One night he said, "Let's take a ride. I have to meet this guy. I have to get some coins and stamps he's selling."

So I took a ride and I sat in the car across the street from the lot where the guy was parked. Greg went into the other guy's car. I saw him put his arm around the guy; then, all of a sudden, I heard *"boom, boom."* He shot him in the head and just took the stamps and the coins. He wasn't paying for them. Then he came back to the car like nothing happened. He was all smiles. But that was Greg. I think his adrenaline went up when he killed somebody.

I was always with Greg. If he had to meet someone, I would be there. If people came to my house for a meeting or to talk to him, he never told me to go into the other room. In fact, if I got up to leave, he'd say, "Sit down, sweetheart." And I'd sit down. Everyone got used to it. It was like I was one of the boys.

Once Greg and his crew did a robbery at an airport—it was jewelry. Greg said they had to bring the stuff back to the house. I said sure, as long as he gave me something. So the guys came over with these big airport bags and laid all the jewelry out on the table. Greg gave me whatever I wanted.

Even though I knew what he did, I never thought Greg would get arrested. I never thought he'd get shot. I never thought he would die. It just wasn't in my head, none of that stuff, because he had a lot of backing from the FBI. I felt very secure with Greg, and I think Greg felt secure, too, because he just did what he wanted. I mean there was nothing he wouldn't do. And the FBI knew about it before he did it. Greg lived the gangster life. He'd go out killing people or robbing banks, robbing airports or trucks. And he'd talk to the FBI.

After we dated for a while, I knew I wanted to have kids with Greg. I wanted my own family, my own kids. But in those days, you didn't have kids without getting married—and Greg was already married. I didn't want to hurt my father by doing that, so I talked to Greg about it.

"Listen, I'm going to just meet somebody and marry him. Then we can have kids now, until we can move in together. I don't want to have kids without being married."

"No, what are you crazy? We just move in. We'll get an apartment."

I told him I couldn't do that to my father, so I married this nice guy named Charlie. I lived with Charlie until I had Joey. Then two or three months after Joey was born, Charlie left; and then a little while after that, Greg moved in.

I grew up thinking Charlie was my real father. At that time—I was born in 1969 and Joey came along a couple years later—having a baby without being married just wasn't done. My mother's marriage to Charlie ultimately ended—they eventually divorced—and Greg moved in with us, but I still called Charlie my father.

Until I was about four or five years old, we lived with Charlie in Brooklyn. We lived on Fifty-Fifth Street, between Seventeenth and Eighteenth Avenues. I didn't remember exactly when Greg came into the house because I was so young. I just remember that it was Charlie; then, all of a sudden, it was Greg because Greg was always part of our lives.

I called him "Greggy" at the time—I didn't call him "Dad." I called Charlie my dad, and so did my brother. But we were really confused. We didn't understand why Greg was in the house acting like a daddy, but then we also had Charlie, who was Daddy.

My father had another family—his wife, Connie, and four kids: Deborah, the oldest, Greg Junior, the second oldest, Bart and Frankie, the youngest. When my father separated from Connie, she and the kids lived in New Jersey.

I called Greg Junior, "Gregory." He was about twenty years older than me. In the beginning I didn't know he was my brother because I didn't know Greg Senior was my father. But Gregory was very good to me. He acted fatherly toward me. He used to call me "dollface," and he always gave me hugs and kisses. He was very affectionate like a family member would be—and that just confused me even more.

We asked a lot of questions, but my parents—Greg and my mother—didn't really make it easy for us.

"Well, Charlie is your dad. You have to see him every other Sunday, or every Sunday—whenever else you want, you could see him. But you see him on Sundays," my mother said.

Even so, Greg acted like a real father in the house. He put us to bed, helped us with homework—all the things fathers did. Except for Sundays when Charlie picked us up. But the fact was even when we were young, we were being taught that Greg was in charge.

"Something happens, you tell me, and I'll take care of it," he told us.

When my little brother, Joey, was about four, he got into a fight with another young boy. The kid bullied my brother, and my brother came home crying.

"What happened, Joey?" my father asked.

My brother told him that this kid had bothered him. My father went into his bedroom and came out holding a baseball bat.

"Okay, take this bat and hit him over the head with the bat, and then when he's crying, tell him to go get his father."

He was telling this to a little four-year-old. So my

brother went out to do what my father told him to do. But Joey made up with the other little boy and didn't end up hitting him.

Most of the time growing up on Fifty-Fifth Street was pretty normal. My father used to watch TV with us and play video games. He was a regular dad. Taking care of us when we got hurt or when we were sick.

One day I was playing outside and I fell and hurt my knee. I was screaming like somebody was killing me. My father came running out of the house because I was yelling at the top of my lungs. He jumped over the patio, thinking I must have been really injured. And there I was, with a little scratch on my knee.

He picked me up and said, "Oh. What happened, my baby? You got a little boo-boo." But meanwhile he was having a heart attack because he thought something really bad had happened to me.

Another time I was extremely sick. I had such a high fever and my father and my mother couldn't bring it down. They took me into the bathroom to put me in a cool bath. I was crying and screaming and my fever just kept getting higher and higher. My father couldn't deal with the stress. He got so crazy that he actually punched himself in the head, knocked himself out and fell into the tub. He literally knocked himself out.

One summer after dinner I was playing on the front steps with my toys. I was ready for bed, wearing my Winnie-the-Pooh pajamas. I was about six. My father came outside to tell me it was time to come in. We started talking and sometime during the conversation I called him "Dad." I caught myself.

"Oh, I mean Greggy."

"It's okay, honey. You can call me 'Daddy.'"

"Okay, Greggy."

But I still wasn't sure. Most of the time, I called him Greggy. But every once in a while I'd call him Daddy, and he loved it. He'd always tell me it was okay to call him Daddy. I think the day I first called him Daddy was the happiest day of his life.

Then I started getting used to calling him Daddy, even though I didn't really think he was my dad. He felt like my dad, but at the time Charlie was really still my dad. I never let Charlie know that I called Greg, Dad. So whenever I visited Charlie, I always had to say Greg. I knew that I couldn't refer to Greg as Daddy in front of Charlie. I was just a little kid. It was very confusing and I was very torn.

Sometimes when my parents went out, our neighbors, Maria and Louis, used to take care of us. I hated it—I didn't like just anybody else taking care of us. I wanted my mother and my father home. At that point I had started to think of Greg as another father.

One day when they were babysitting us, I was watching a movie. In the movie the girl's father died. When my parents came home, I was crying my eyes out.

"What's the matter?" my father asked, sitting down on the couch with me.

"Are you going to die?"

"Why are you asking that?"

"Because I saw a movie, and the girl's daddy died. Are you going to die?"

"I'm not going anywhere." He always used to tell me that and I really believed him, up until I was in my twenties. I didn't want anything to happen to my father.

Once when I was young, he came home with bruises on his arms. I asked what had happened, and he told me that the bad policeman did that to him. I asked why and he said because policemen weren't nice.

Not long after that, I was driving in the car with my mother, and a police cruiser pulled up next to my side of the car when we were stopped at a red light. The policemen looked over at me and started waving. I opened my window and yelled at them.

"You're bad. You hurt my daddy. I don't like you."

My mother was horrified.

"Oh, my God. I'm so sorry. She doesn't know what she's saying. She didn't mean that."

The cops didn't know what to think because here was this sweet-looking little girl yelling at them, telling them that she didn't like them because they hurt her daddy.

During this time my father was running his crew from the Wimpy Boys Social Club on Thirteenth Avenue in Bensonhurst, an old Italian neighborhood in the heart of Brooklyn. The club moved to a second location on Thirteenth Avenue later, but I really didn't go there much.

Back in the day there were Mob-run "social clubs" from different crime families on almost every avenue in Brooklyn. My father's name for his club was, of course, ironic because "wimpy" was the exact opposite of what they all were.

There were about thirty guys in his crew, either full-blooded Italian or of partial Italian descent. Some were made men, while others were young associates—mobsters in training hoping to become members of the Colombo crime family.

There were Mob guys everywhere. They would just hang outside—sometimes on lounge chairs— drinking and smoking cigarettes. Everything was so open back then and everybody was just so free-spirited. No one was thinking about the cops. That's just the way it was. That's how I remember Brooklyn.

My father usually left the house at 11 A.M. to go to the club and he'd be back by 5 P.M. for dinner. We all had to be in the house by that time and have dinner together. Dinner was at five, every day. He left whatever he was doing at the club to be home with us.

No matter what they had going on—card games, whatever—he'd tell his crew: "Time for me to go." If he wanted to have a talk with the members of his crew after dinner, they would have to come to the house. It was very rare that he went back out after dinner, unless he was going out with my mother.

But during the day the social club was where they met to talk business, take care of business and play cards. They ran numbers from the club, gambled and lent money; I'm sure they planned a lot of hits there. The club was the place where they had to show face every day. Like a regular job, they had to be there.

And they all had to be dressed appropriately. They couldn't go there looking like slobs, because my father wanted everybody to be clean-cut. His crew had to look like they were ready to do business, not like they were ready to hang out in the streets. My father was very strict about it.

A friend of mine, Sal, who used to hang out there, told me that he went to the club one day without shaving. My brother Greg told him he had to go home.

"Why do I have to go home?" Sal asked.

"When you come back with a clean shave, you can come in the club," Greg said. "But until then you have to go."

When we were kids, my mother used to drive Joey and me to the club if she had to see my father. We were really young, but I remember that it had wood paneling and carpeting and my father's office was in the back.

Whenever my brother and I used to walk in there—I was about eight or nine, and Joey was about six or seven—the guys would all give us money. Well, actually, they'd give me money; they used to make Joey work for it.

My brother took gymnastics and he was good at it. He used to walk on his hands. He could walk across a room—and even walk down steps—on his hands. The guys would say to Joey, "I'm going to bet you that you can't walk from this side of the club to the other side of the club."

"I can do it! I can do it," Joey would say.

"All right, twenty dollars if you can do it."

"Well, if I walk back and forth, then I want double."

By the time Joey walked out of the club when it

was time to go home, he'd have $50 or more. Joey loved going there because it was such fun for him—most of the time.

My father's friend "Scappy"—Colombo capo Anthony Scarpati and my father's "boss"—was the one who always bet my brother couldn't walk on his hands across the club. Scappy was always teasing my brother. He'd give him a wedgie or just do things to annoy him. It was okay if it was in good fun, but my father didn't like anybody teasing Joey or me.

One day Scappy put ice cubes down the front of my brother's pants. Joey got really upset and started crying. My father yelled at Scappy and told him never to do that to Joey again, which was crazy because Scappy was the boss. But Scappy never did it again. The truth is that Scappy treated us unbelievably well, but he just liked to tease my brother. And my father didn't like that at all.

We loved going to the club because there was a candy store right across the street—we used to say it was our candy store because we could get anything we wanted and we never had to pay for it. Then there was the luncheonette next door. When we visited my father, he'd take us there for breakfast or just to get a couple milk shakes.

They also had those chocolate egg creams, although there weren't any eggs in them. They were made with milk or half-and-half and soda water and either vanilla or chocolate syrup. Egg creams were big in Brooklyn because it was rumored that the guy who invented them came from the neighborhood. We loved going to the club because we could go to the luncheonette and sit with my father for a while.

That old club had a warm feeling to it, but the new club was kind of cold. We really didn't like it. What I remember most about the new club was the steps going downstairs. You didn't ever want to go down those steps. Well, if you were a guy, you didn't want to take the walk down those steps because you were going to get a beating or worse. We were never allowed down the steps.

You could see my father's office as soon as you walked in, so he had two-way glass installed. He could see out, but nobody could see in. I always thought it was pretty cool. As I got older, I realized why that was necessary.

Joey didn't like it at that club because now that he was older, he really didn't like some of the guys. Joey told my father that he didn't want any part of them. And that's the way he felt throughout his life.

CHAPTER 3

DO YOU KNOW WHO YOUR FATHER IS?

We lived in the house on Fifty-Fifth Street until I was around seven; then we moved to Avenue J in Brooklyn. We moved because my parents found a better house, plus we were on a dead-end block on Fifty-Fifth. My father didn't like living on a dead-end block—he felt he didn't have a way out. If anything went down, he would have been trapped.

Our first experience on Avenue J was when the kids around the block started throwing mud balls at me and my brother. My father had to go and talk to their fathers. That was our first day there. We were miserable; we hated living there at first. But things eventually got better.

Although I hated the neighborhood, I loved our house on Avenue J, especially my room. I had pictures of all the hot movie and TV stars tacked up on my walls: John Stamos and Scott Baio—Chachi from *Happy Days*—I loved him. He was all over my room. I always had beautiful furniture in my room. It was Formica back then, but it was all white Formica.

The rest of the house was mainly brown and white—my mother's favorite colors. We had bamboo wallpaper and brown furniture. Really fancy furniture, big wall units, the best TVs and sound systems. We had the most up-to-date gadgets in the kitchen—things other people didn't have, except my father's friends. Whatever was new, we had it in the house. We even had a tanning room in the basement.

Our house was always the place where everyone wanted to be. My father was a very big family man, and he was very into holidays and birthdays. His friends, their wives or girlfriends, my aunts, uncles and cousins all came to the house on Avenue J for Thanksgiving and Christmas. We had a huge table. My father and mother did most of the cooking. My brother and I couldn't wait for the holidays. It was the best time for us. The Christmas gifts, the people and the parties—it was just so much fun. There was such a feeling of warmth.

We had a very welcoming house. My father would make breakfast for his friends if they came to the house in the morning. There was always coffee brewing; pancakes, sausages and eggs cooking on the stove. My father was just like a regular father and a regular guy who loved his family and friends.

Our house was always filled with people. My parents liked to party. They were always having parties at the house. They also enjoyed getting all dressed up to go out drinking. They were completely different from the parents of my friends at school. I never thought of my father as a typical guy who worked a 9-to-5 job and then came home to his family.

My father's crew was always in and out of the house—even when we lived on Fifty-Fifth Street. At first, I just thought they were his friends. They were so nice to me. They'd pick me up and swing me around. They'd hug and kiss me. And they'd always buy me gifts. To me, they were the greatest people in the world. My mother hung out with their wives or girlfriends—or their wives and their girlfriends—and I didn't really understand that, either.

My father and his friends weren't like everyone else. Most members of my father's crew were pretty good-looking. Those guys were charming. Flashy dressers, with nice cars and nice jewelry. They smelled nice, wearing cologne like Grey Flannel. They always wore sunglasses—even at night. All the guys, including my father, shopped at the George Richland men's clothing store in Bensonhurst. They all wore leisure suits, seamless dress pants and patent leather shoes. Some of them even had their initials embroidered on their shirts. I never saw any of this going on in other people's houses.

Joey and I loved his friends, too. They were so different from other people. And they treated us like we were really special. Everybody treated us very warmly—we had a lot of love from a lot of people. We had the best time of our lives on Avenue J because of the family and the friends—my father's friends, not our friends—and all the get-togethers.

For a long time, though, we were confused about

what my father was and what he did. He was a professional gambler. He owned a restaurant. He came up with different stories all the time.

Finally, one day, I just asked.

"Dad, when people ask me what you do, like at career day at school, what do I say?"

"Just tell them that I'm a professional gambler."

"A professional gambler, what the heck is that?"

"Linda, that's a real job. People do gamble professionally."

So whenever anybody asked what my father did for a living, I'd tell them that he was a professional gambler. They'd just sort of look at me. At that point, I didn't really know any better. My brother and I just went with it. What choice did we have? Maybe we weren't sure what he did for work at first, but one thing we did know for sure was that the love that my father showed us was unconditional—at least before all the violence started.

My father pretty much kept us sheltered until we were teenagers. We had really strict rules. Not only did we have to have dinner at a certain time, but we had to be in bed by a certain time—9:30 P.M. when we were younger, unless we were watching a special show as a family, and then eleven o'clock or midnight when we were in high school.

But even though we were in bed, it didn't mean we'd go to sleep. Sometimes when we were younger, I'd sneak into Joey's room or he'd sneak into mine. A lot of times we heard noises coming from my parents' room—music and laughing. That's just the way they were—very into each other. So we'd sneak up to their door and try to hear what was going on.

"Lin, what are they doing?" Joey would ask because we really didn't know.

As we got older, and I started to figure things out, I'd tell my dad, "Me and Joey heard you and Mom making a lot of noise last night and we couldn't sleep."

Then my father would say, "Really. What did you hear?"

"I don't know. We just heard you making a lot of noise, Dad. And your hair looks kind of messy this morning."

They didn't really hide things like that. They weren't the type of parents who were discreet. My mother and father were very open. Joey and I didn't really like it, but what could we do?

In a lot of ways we were the typical family, spending time together, going on vacation. When we were younger, we went on a lot of vacations to Florida with my mother. My father came with us sometimes, but often we went with people in my father's crew, such as Joseph "Joe Brewster" DeDomenico—I really loved Joe Brewster—and Robert "Bobby Zam" Zambardi. I was about seven or eight years old. I always thought it was weird that they came with us.

When I got older, my mother told me why they were with us—they were going there to kill people. Sometimes we'd all go down there first to check things out, like where they were going to do the actual murder.

One time we drove down because they were going to kill this guy named Joe Peraino, but they didn't get the job done. Joe Brewster had the gun in his shorts, but he must have forgotten about it because he went swimming and he lost it in the ocean. So we just flew back to New York. I got my first airline pin from the pilot on that trip.

When Larry Mazza came into the picture, I was around ten and Joey was about eight. Larry was my mother's lover. We didn't know that until we were much older. He was eighteen and she was thirty-two when they first got together. My father knew about it and he was okay with it. In fact, Larry became part of the family. That was strange for me and my brother at the time because we weren't really sure who this guy was. After a while, though, having him around became second nature to us.

Larry was this really handsome man—tan, good-looking, well-spoken, was polished. He had this way about him. Because he was young, he didn't seem like the other guys who were hanging around with my father.

He was so cute and I had a kiddie crush on him. Whenever he came to the house, I always wanted to sit next to him. My mother told me I was too young to be looking at boys.

Larry was around the house more than anybody else, even Greg Junior. He had a very positive influence on us. Larry just cared about our best interests. He never wanted to see anything bad happen to me or to my brother when we were young. He was like a big brother, and Joey needed that because he was very shy.

Joey loved Larry. He made Larry his sponsor for his Confirmation and he took Larry's name as his Confirmation name. Because we went to Catholic school, Confirmation was a big deal back then; it was also a big deal that Joey picked Larry to be his sponsor over everyone else.

To help Joey overcome his shyness, Larry said he wanted to get him involved in karate and self-defense to build his confidence. Larry was a black belt and he felt that karate would be the best thing for Joey. Larry played a big part in helping my brother come out of his shell and learn to be more sociable.

My brother did really well in karate. His teacher absolutely adored him. He said Joey was one of his best students and he had so much potential. Joey loved karate. He lived for it. He walked around the house in his karate pants and belt. He used to watch the *Karate Kid* over and over and over again. He'd imitate the Karate Kid's stance just to annoy you. He'd stand in front of you with his hands out and one leg up and he'd be making all the karate sounds. It was pretty funny.

He participated in competitions, which was a big thing for him because he was so shy and not able to express himself. So for him to go out there and compete, it was a big deal. Martial arts is all about respect and discipline and hard work, and Joey was taught to walk away from trouble and only to fight to defend himself.

So when his teacher found out that Larry was involved with my father, he told Larry that he wasn't allowed at the school anymore. So Larry took Joey to his lessons, but he couldn't go inside with him. But even so, Larry and karate really helped Joey when he was younger.

Joey stopped taking lessons when we moved to

Eighty-Second Street when he was about fourteen. As soon as he got to high school at Bishop Ford, he started having trouble. He was failing. He was miserable in that school.

He was really having a problem with the principal, Mr. Fernandez. For some reason the principal didn't like Joey. He didn't treat Joey right. He had some gripe with Joey, but I think the gripe was really with my father. Everyone in that school treated us differently than they treated everyone else. I think the teachers knew who my father was—at that point, so did we.

My parents took Joey out of Bishop Ford and put him in a public high school, where he did better. It was either that or the principal at Bishop Ford was going to be found dead in his office.

I didn't do so well in school. I had a problem with learning. I kept telling the teachers that I had a learning disability. But Catholic-school teachers, back then especially, they didn't really care about that. Maybe because they didn't know too much about it. They didn't address my disability, so I struggled in school with comprehension and learning in general.

Larry was very into school and he helped us with our homework. He tried hard to help me with my assignments, but I couldn't understand anything. I never got diagnosed, so I never knew the exact problem.

By the time I was a teenager, a lot of the kids around Avenue J were drinking and experimenting with drugs. The kids in that neighborhood didn't really like me and there were a lot of bullies there. But I still had the girlfriends—especially three really close friends—I made at the Holy Ghost School. I went there from the first to the eighth grade. We used to have so much fun. There were lots of sleepovers and parties. The Halloween parties were great.

When I look back, I kind of understand why the kids on Avenue J, particularly the girls, didn't like me. I always had the best of everything. I was the one pulling up to school in a limo. I had the best clothes. If I had a pair of boots, I had them in ten colors. Most of the other girls in the neighborhood were kind of poor and they hated me. But I didn't know any different—it was my life. I guess that's why I really didn't have any female friends when we lived on Avenue J. The friends I had were mainly boys.

It was different for my brother. Joey wasn't too much of an experimental type of kid. He was more into school. He had friends on the block. He was more sociable than I was when we got older—karate had really helped. I was more introverted and he became much friendlier. It was the exact opposite of what it was like when we were kids.

When I was about thirteen or so, I started hanging out with the experimental crew, and I decided to be experimental. It was the early 1980s. Pot was the thing. I was hanging out with these guys and a couple girls from a different neighborhood, around Twentieth Avenue. It wasn't too far from where we lived. So I'd walk there after school. We used to hang out in a schoolyard and smoke pot. Then we'd play video games in a nearby candy store. I was having a ball. It was fun and I was loving it.

My curfew was 9 P.M. I was still kind of young to be out that late, but my father always told me he trusted me. But as soon as my father let me go a little, I let go a lot. When he gave me that trust, then he lost me because I was really too young.

"I'll give you a lot of rope, and I'll give you all the trust in the world," he told me. "But once you break it, then you're going to have a problem with me."

He allowed me go out with my friends, but I had to be home by curfew. One particular night, I didn't realize what time it was and I smoked pot way too close to curfew. I was really high. So I went to my friend Argie's house. I needed someone to pick me up, but I didn't want to call the house. So I called Larry. When Larry got to Argie's, he just looked at me.

"Linda, are you okay?"

"Yeah, why?"

"You don't look so good."

"Well, I'm fine. What do you mean?"

Meanwhile, I couldn't even talk—my mouth was like cotton mouth and my tongue was numb.

"Are you sure you want me to take you home right now?"

"Yeah, take me home. There's no problem."

I was brain-dead at that point. I didn't even understand what was going on around me. Everything was a joke.

"Okay, but are you sure?"

"Yeah, take me home. What are you looking at, anyway?"

Here was Larry trying to help me and I was being a little brat.

When I walked into the house, I knew I was pretty messed up. Usually when I walked in, the first thing I did was say hi to my parents and ask them what they were watching. The family room was the first room you walked into, so there was no way around seeing them.

That night I walked right past both of them. I ran downstairs into the bathroom and locked the door. I looked at myself in the mirror. My pupils were huge and my eyes were bloodshot. *Oh, my God, I'm dead.*

I turned the water on and grabbed the soap. I figured I'd wash my face and tell them I got soap in my eyes. Then I heard my mother stomping down the stairs. She started pounding on the bathroom door and screaming.

"Linda, open the door!"

"Wait a second. I'm washing my face."

"Open the door . . . now."

"I'm washing my face." I could hardly talk, so everything was coming out all garbled. I finally opened the door. I was wiping my face.

"You know, you made me get soap in my eyes."

She took one look at me and screamed for my father. I couldn't believe she was doing that to me. *Boom. Boom. Boom.* He was running down the steps so fast. The minute he saw me, he said, "She's high."

"No, I'm not. Really." I was so messed up, it sounded like I was talking in a different language.

"She can't even talk. What did you take?"

"Dad, I didn't take anything." I was so stoned. I was talking gibberish and they couldn't understand me. I must've smoked some heavy shit that night.

I kept trying to convince them that I wasn't high, but they kept screaming at me and saying, "Oh, my God." They were having this conversation about me, but I couldn't understand it. I was just standing there looking at them. I couldn't believe it was happening. Everything around me was moving at crazy-fast speeds and my brain was working in slow motion.

I knew I was really dead at that point, so I figured I had nothing to lose.

"I hate you. I hate you both."

"Who were you with? We want to know who you were with."

"I'm not telling you anything."

"Look at her, she can't even talk," my father said. He was getting really pissed because now they knew I was high.

"You little bitch, you're dead," my mother said.

"Shut up."

I was really pissed at my mother, so I was fighting with her. I tried to make a run for it up the stairs. But my father put his foot out. I wasn't sure what he was trying to do, because I was stoned. Maybe he was trying to stop me. All I knew was that he put his foot out, and I thought he tried to kick me because he was mad. I didn't understand because he had never raised a hand to me, *ever*. I was so mad—I started screaming at them.

"I hate you! I don't want anything to do with either one of you. This is your fault because you people make me live a crazy life, and I don't want anything to do with it. I want to go live with my father. I'm calling him right now!"

They weren't about to let me get away with that.

"That's it, you're punished. You're not allowed out of this house. We're going to find out everybody you were with," my father said.

"I'm calling my father. I want to be with him. I don't want to live with you two. I hate you."

Right about then, I started to sober up. Maybe it was the shock of everything, but I was beginning to wake up out of it.

But I just kept screaming at my father: "I hate you! I hate you! Don't tell me what to do. You're not even my father."

As soon as I got those words out, my father started to cry.

"I'm your father. I'm your father."

"No, you're not. You're not my father. Charlie is my father."

"Linda, I'm your father. I've always been your father. There's been no one else but me. It's always been me."

"What are you talking about? What are you talking about now? You're not my father. I don't understand what you're saying."

Then my mother started to explain.

"Listen, we never told you because we didn't want to upset you or confuse you."

"You don't want to confuse me? What are you talking about?"

"Well, Charlie is really not your father, okay? Charlie is not your father. So don't think you're going to call Charlie," my mother said.

"Right. You're just saying this because you don't want me to call Charlie and live with Charlie. This is bullshit."

"No, this is the truth."

And then my father told me the whole story about why my mother married Charlie. I was thinking about what he was telling me, but I didn't want to hear anything else. I was still fighting them.

"I'm still calling Charlie. I don't even believe you. I don't even know what you're talking about."

"Listen, go wherever you have to go," my father said.

"You guys are really crazy. And then you wonder why I'm getting high. I want to get high right now. I don't understand why you guys are telling me this. I don't understand you people."

I was in total shock. My mind was racing a mile a minute. They were telling me this whole crazy story. Was it true? I didn't really look like Charlie. I didn't have any idea what they were talking about. My head was rocking. I couldn't take any more. I had to go to sleep. I told my parents I was going to bed and I didn't care what they were doing. Finally they went back upstairs.

I had no idea why they decided to tell me Greg was my father then. They must have been in shock, too—seeing me so high that they felt they had to rationalize the way we were living. Maybe they felt guilty because of what I did. Maybe they were thinking they had to tell me the truth so I would stop doing drugs and get back on the right track.

The only thing I could think of was that my words hurt my father so bad because he loved me so much. A day didn't go by in my father's life that I didn't tell him I loved him—even when I thought Charlie was my real father—not one day. I told him I loved him at least ten times a day. And every night before he went to bed, or before I went to bed, I'd kiss him and say, "I love you. I love you, Dad. I love you so much."

So for him to see me high—and for me to be screaming, "It's your fault. I hate you"—was the breaking point and he had to tell me the truth. But at that moment I didn't care. I hated him. And he made me hate him even more the following day.

I crashed on the couch in the basement that night. I woke up the next morning and I heard them upstairs in the kitchen. Then I started remembering everything. I was really scared. I knew I was *so* dead. I didn't want to go upstairs because I didn't want to deal with it.

Then I heard, "Linda, get up here." *Oh, my God. My father.*

I went upstairs and he gave me the whole speech about drugs.

"You're punished. You're not allowed out of the house. You're not allowed to hang out with those people. We're going to find out who you were with."

I couldn't get a word in. I had no idea what was going to happen, but I had to play it cool.

"Whatever."

I knew I was in trouble. I thought the kids I was with were in trouble. But never—not for one minute—did I think he was going to do what he did.

My parents knew who I hung out with, so my mother called the mother of one of the girls in the group.

"My daughter was with your daughter last night and they smoked pot." My mother didn't know for sure, but she figured she could get some information.

"Not my daughter, she don't do that." There really wasn't anything they could do to the girl, anyway, so my mother just yelled and screamed at the lady.

Then my father went out with some of his crew and somehow they found out that I had been smoking pot with my best friend, Greg Vacca. I loved him then, and I still love him. We used to hang out every day. I guess you could say he was my first boyfriend.

Next thing I knew, my father came back to the house.

"Guess what? You want to smoke pot? Now your friends pay the price, and you don't have friends anymore. You're not allowed to hang out with them anymore."

I started screaming. "What do you mean, my friends 'pay the price'? What did you do? What did you do?"

"Don't worry about it. It's not for you to know."

"What do you mean, it's not for me to know? I want to know what you did."

Of course, I cared about the other people, but I didn't care about them as much as I cared about Greg. My father knew that. So, who did he go after? He went after the guy I hung out with the most. Greg was my buddy, and he caught the beating of his life. He was only sixteen.

I didn't even have a chance to warn him, because I didn't know what was going to happen. He was walking in the neighborhood and my father and his crew picked him up and put him in the car. They beat the living daylights out of him and then literally dropped him on the side of the road.

I didn't want to hear anything about it, so I ran upstairs to my room. A little while later the doorbell rang. After a while my father yelled for me to come downstairs. When I did, I saw Greg and his father sitting in the living room.

When I saw Greg, I almost died. My heart was broken. He just glared at me. He gave me such a nasty look. He thought I told on him, but I didn't. I didn't tell my parents anything about what had happened that night.

Greg was just sitting there. I couldn't bear to look at him. His head was misshapen. There were bumps the size of grapefruits. His eyes were completely shut except for these little slits. His lips . . . I didn't even know how they stayed formed. I don't know how he survived that beating.

Greg's father knew my father, and he knew what my father did, but he didn't care. His son had been beaten up so badly that he wanted to kill my father. Greg's father wanted to know how my father could beat up a sixteen-year-old boy.

"Listen, I don't give a fuck what you say, this is what he did."

"What do you mean, this is what he did? Your daughter was smoking, too."

"I don't care. He should know better. He's older than her. He knows who I am. He knows what's going to happen to him if they get caught. So, why would he go and smoke pot with her?"

I knew that my father wasn't a regular guy. He was a street guy, but I didn't know he was a full-fledged gangster. I didn't yet understand the concept of "gangster." What he meant was that people in the neighborhood knew who he was. Greg knew my father was a scary guy, but did he know my father was in the Colombo crime family? No, probably not.

My father and Greg's father kept going at it. Greg's dad didn't hold back what he had to say. I gave him credit for that—he was pissed off and held his ground. But he knew there was nothing he could do. What was he going to do? Call the cops? And then what?

Finally Greg and his father left. It was just my father and me. I was traumatized. I couldn't stop crying.

"I hate you. How could you hurt Greg like that? Of all the people. Of all my friends. How could you do that to him?"

He just looked at me.

"That's what happens when you do stupid things. Maybe next time, you won't do stupid things."

I felt terrible. My father made me think it was my fault. I was miserable and depressed over that for a very long time. I cried for Greg. For him and for me. I really didn't have a lot of friends, and I lost my best friend. He hated me after that—hated me. We didn't talk for years. I lost all the other friends I hung out with, too. They knew somebody got beat up because of me.

I sat on my stoop—it seemed like forever—waiting for him to come by so I could talk to him. I wasn't walking the streets anymore.

One day I saw him and I tried to talk to him.

He looked at me with such hate.

"Don't ever come near me again."

"But I didn't tell him."

"Then how did he know?"

"He just knew. If he didn't know, he was going to

beat you up, anyway, and try to find out. I had no say in it."

My father knew Greg was my closest friend, so Greg was the one who was going to get it. That's just the way it was.

The whole neighborhood where I hung out hated me after that—the whole neighborhood. I couldn't hang there ever again. All I could do was stay in my house. The girls in that neighborhood all wanted to beat me up. They didn't care who my family was— not that they really knew at that age—but they didn't care that my father was a scary guy.

There was this big girl, and her name was "Fat Karen." She came up to me one day when I was sitting on the stoop and hit me in the face with a closed fist. My father and mother heard me scream and ran outside. My father almost hit her—he never hit women—because she hurt me. My mother had to grab his arm.

Growing up, I always felt that nobody liked me. I figured I must be ugly because nobody wanted to talk to me. A couple years after all this happened, I asked my father about it.

"Dad, nobody likes me. Am I ugly?"

"Linda, do you know who your father is? Do you know who I am?"

"What does that mean? What does that have to do with what I'm telling you, Dad?"

"Linda, they're afraid of you because of me."

Then I started to figure out that he was in the Mob. I was getting older, and it just made sense. Nobody ever said, "Your father is a gangster" or "Your father is in the Mob." But as I got older, I got smarter.

I knew that he wasn't a professional gambler. He was a violent guy out on the street. I didn't get the whole Colombo crime family thing yet, but I did know that people feared him.

I never really got over what my father did to Greg. It stayed with me for a very long time. I ran into Greg when we were adults and we became friends again. I apologized to him a thousand times.

He said he didn't hate me anymore. "Linda, I was just a kid getting beat up by men. I don't know how I lived."

CHAPTER 4

TURN YOUR WOUNDS INTO WISDOM

When I told Greg Vacca I was writing a book and I was going to include what my father did to him, he started telling me the whole story from his perspective. He reminded me of things I guess I forgot about, or maybe subconsciously didn't want to remember. His story is so powerful that I decided to ask him to tell you about it in his own words.

I was celebrating my sixteenth birthday with the guys I always hung around with—there were about five of them. We decided to have a little party in this apartment we had rigged up downstairs in an abandoned building in Brooklyn. It used to be the super's apartment. We rigged it up with electricity and everything.

We had a secret entrance. To get down to the

basement, you had to go around the side of the building in the back. There was a basement window that was all boarded up. We would take the boards on the outside off, but when we got inside, we would put the boards back up on the inside so the window still looked boarded up.

We decided to have Linda and one of her friends meet up with us there to party. When she arrived, she came up to wish me a happy birthday. Then she gave me a cigarette pack about half full of joints. It was just what I wanted. I asked her where they came from and she told me she took them from her dad.

Linda really wasn't an experienced pot smoker like us. She had tried it a few times, but she really wasn't doing it right. So that night she started smoking, and she still wasn't doing it right. I told her, "You've got to inhale it." But when she inhaled, she basically coughed her brains out. She nearly puked, but she said she was okay.

We smoked for most of the night. Then she said it was getting close to her curfew so she was going home. I tried to talk her out of it.

"Linda, do not go home like that. Your father is going to pin you out right away."

I knew her father was involved with the Mafia, but I didn't know how much he was involved.

"No, I'll be all right. I'm going to go to Argie's house."

Argie was one of our friends. Argie's parents, especially her father, were really strict, too. I didn't really like him. So Linda left and we continued our party. Linda didn't come back, so I figured she must have made it home okay.

But when I got home, my parents were on the phone with Linda's parents. They were pretty much going at it on the phone. I found out that Larry had picked Linda up at Argie's and took her home. And her father pinned her out, just as I thought he would. So I got in trouble. I was pretty pissed at Linda because I was convinced that she had ratted me out to her father.

The next day my friends and I were supposed to meet at the indoor Avenue I Flea Market in Brooklyn and then play a game of softball. I was a huge baseball player.

We used to go to the flea market and party in the basement. We used to get in through this staircase that was pretty much broken down. We used to squeeze through the fence and go back there. We were crazy. We would party in places where nobody would even think of going.

My friends and I got wasted and then we decided to go upstairs to the flea market. While we were there, I saw Linda and her mother shopping, but Linda didn't look too happy. Linda's mother and I got into an argument. She called me a pothead and said I made her daughter do this and that. But that wasn't the case—I didn't make her do anything. And that's just what I told her mother.

"Who are you calling a pothead? I didn't make her do anything. She got the weed from you guys, so look who's talking."

Big Linda was pissed because I pretty much embarrassed her in front of all the people at the flea market. That's when she grabbed me by the arm and started shaking me. I sort of pushed her arm off me, but I didn't push her. She took a couple steps back and started screaming at me. "You just wait," she said.

We were yelling back and forth. I never started any fights, but I wasn't a guy you wanted to pick a fight with. Then Linda and her mother left.

My friends and I started walking around the flea market. We were stoned as hell. Then next thing I knew, these two guys came out of nowhere and one of them hit one of my friends in the face. He just jabbed him out.

These guys weren't dressed like us; they were dressed like gangsters. It was a Saturday or Sunday morning and we were in softball gear and they were wearing Capezios—and when I think about it now— looking like Don Johnson in *Miami Vice*. So I was thinking these guys weren't just street thugs.

We started to retaliate and we ended up chasing them out of the flea market. When we got outside, the guys ran over to their car and I saw Linda and her mother in the backseat. My friend Stephen threw a baseball bat at the guys. It hit the back window of the car, shattering the glass. The last thing I heard before the car took off was Linda's mother scream-ing at me out the window, "You wait until tonight!"

After that, we went to play softball and everything seemed fine. Later on that night, I was at our apart-ment building hangout with my group, and we were partying as usual. We ran out of pot, but we knew some guys who used to sell weed at the bowling alley on Avenue I, about two blocks away. It was raining that night; so since I was the most athletic and the fastest, I said, "I'll go get it. I'll run."

So my friends gave me the money. I'm trucking myself along, and about a block or so away, I see three cars with a lot of guys in them—there must have been ten or twelve guys—on the other side of the street. It didn't look right, but I kept running and didn't think any more about it.

Then, all of a sudden, a car pulled up next to me. There was a used-car lot on the other side, and there was a big fence. Behind the fence were Dobermans and other guard dogs, so I couldn't escape that way.

Then one car pulled up behind me and one in front of me. They pretty much boxed me in. I tried to jump over the hood of the car, but it was raining. I made it, but when I hit the roof, I slipped.

The guys were out of the cars by that point. One of them grabbed my leg, and I fell on my head. And they just friggin' pulverized me. They annihilated me. I ended up with a broken nose, a concussion, two fractured ribs, and the rest of my whole body was bruised everywhere. And my head was so swollen, I looked like the Elephant Man. It was pretty bad. These were grown men. They were dressed like gangsters and they all had guns. I was only sixteen.

When they first got me, they beat me up outside. It started getting a little out of hand, so they threw me in one of the cars and drove across the street to a pretty secluded gas station. Linda's father was in the driver's seat; her brother Greg was in the front passenger seat; I was in the backseat, in the middle, with a guy on each side holding me.

Her father turned around and hit me a few times. He had a good punch—he had a better punch than her brother. I tried moving my head to head butt Greg Junior's hand. I was pretty sure I hurt his hand, because I moved my face out of the way. I took boxing when I was a kid, and they taught me to move my head and try and break the opponent's hand when it hit me, so that's what I tried to do.

The whole time they were hitting me, her father kept asking me, "Where's Stephen?" They wanted Stephen more than me, but I wouldn't rat. I wouldn't say anything. I just kept telling them that I didn't know.

"Where is he?"

"I don't know."

Boom.

"Where is he?"

"I don't know."

Boom.

This continued on for at least a good ten to fifteen shots.

Finally I said, "I think he's at the bowling alley."

Crack.

"Where is he?"

"I think he's at the bowling alley."

Crack.

But they didn't stop, until I said, "He's at the bowling alley," not "I think he's at the bowling alley." They wanted a definite answer.

These guys then took me from the gas station to the bowling alley, which was about half a block away. It was right on McDonald Avenue, which was famous for being a place where people got killed. When the elevated trains ran overhead, people would blow shots at you and nobody would hear the gunshots.

I was pretty much toast at that point. I was thinking I was dead. But they took me to the bowling alley in search of my friend Stephen. They stood me up outside, and they were bouncing me around the bowling alley wall like I was a pinball. They were smashing me against the wall.

Then they went into the bowling alley. It was a tough place to hang out because another gang of guys hung out there. But Linda's father's crew threw all those guys out when they were looking for Stephen. A couple friends of mine were there and they told me later they didn't know how I survived.

Greg Senior hit me a few times outside. Then he said, "Stephen is not in there." I was thinking that they were going to take me for the ride at that point and finish me off. They're still bouncing me around outside some more. Then Larry Mazza said, "Enough, enough. Come on, enough already."

I knew Larry before he got involved in the Mafia. He was a delivery boy and he used to deliver food to my house. He kept saying, "Enough is enough." But that didn't help. The whole time I was wondering when it was going to end. All I could do was try and make it through.

I wasn't going to rat because I knew they were going to kill Stephen for sure. I knew where he was because I had just left him in that vacant apartment building.

I ended up on the ground, pretty much beaten to a pulp, with my head hanging off the curb. It was still raining and I looked down and saw my blood pouring into a puddle. I was alive probably because I didn't rat my friend out. If I had, they probably would have offed me right there for being a rat. Maybe Linda's father wanted to see how much I could take.

Finally they left. I felt somebody pick me up and pull me into the bowling alley bathroom. He was a pretty high-up guy, so he had his connections, too. He was from a different crew and I think a different family. Other people I knew from the neighborhood had come in and they were taking care of me.

A lot of people knew me. I was the athlete. I did everything. I played baseball—I was a baseball star. I was a musician—I played the drums. I was also a party kid. But I also had a sense of honor. I wasn't the type of guy who would just screw you over for nothing. If you screwed me, I'd get you, but if you didn't, you had no problems with me.

So those guys told me to stay in the bowling alley bathroom and not come out. I guess they were making sure that Linda's father's crew didn't come back hunting for Stephen or me.

After a while, they said it was okay for me to leave the bathroom. I didn't want to leave, though. I was petrified. Finally they took me to my friend's house, and then they took me home.

My mother and sister almost passed out when I walked through the door. They both started crying. My sister had to sit down because she was so hysterical. My father was pissed.

"Who the fuck did this to you?"

I didn't want to tell him because I was scared of what was going to happen; my father had a high-level job with the federal government. But I finally told him.

"Come on, we're going over to the house."

"You're fucking crazy! I'm not going over there. Dad, come on, he's a fucking maniac. He just told me if he ever sees me again, or sees me near his family, he's going to fucking kill me. And I believe him. So, no, I'm not going over there. You're crazy."

"You're fucking going over there with me."

When we got to Linda's house, my father made me stand right outside the door. He rang the bell. Greg came to the door and invited us in. Everything was respectful. My father was pissed, but he was still talking in a respectful manner. For one thing, my father was not dumb. He didn't want to get killed, either.

We were all sitting down on this little couch that was in the front room. My father and Greg were having a sit-down. They came to an agreement.

"Now the agreement is, they stay away from each other, okay? You don't touch my family," my father told Greg. "And I won't touch your family."

And they shook hands on it. That's when Greg called Linda downstairs. I was one of those nice guys. But once you screwed me, forget it. When I got involved with somebody, I really opened up to them. I gave them everything. I felt very betrayed by Linda because I thought she ratted me out to her father. So when she came downstairs, I looked at her pretty much like I hated her.

When Linda saw me, she screamed at her father. "I hate you." And then she ran back upstairs. Then my father and I left.

Before all this happened, Greg liked me. First of all, I had the same name as him and she had the same name as her mother. So it was, "Greg and Linda, Greg and Linda." The fact that he liked me probably saved my life.

I had an eye on Linda from the get-go. She used to come and watch us play softball, and I'd always see her hanging around. I never really talked to her in the beginning. Then I heard about her and her dad. I knew a little bit about that. But what stood out about her was that she really didn't want that whole lifestyle.

She dressed down a lot. She'd wear these little terrycloth sweatpants—nothing fancy or anything that made her look like a little Italian princess. She was so cute, but she looked normal—she always just wanted to look normal. And that's the way she acted.

She was really sweet—a lot sweeter than a typical Brooklyn girl, who would haul off and kick your ass. Linda wasn't like that, although she did have a feisty little temper.

She just kept it very real. My parents liked her because they knew who she was back then. She was a very likable girl, especially by the guys. But the girls didn't like her because they were jealous of her. A lot of those Brooklyn girls wanted that Mob life. And she had it, the minute she was born. But I could tell that she was born into something that she really didn't want.

And her smile was "Oh, my God." That's what I was attracted to about her, besides her beauty. I thought her smile was the best, and still to this day. Out of all the women I've been with in my life, I would say Linda definitely has the best smile. She doesn't do it much, but when she does, it's good.

When we were kids, I was always at Linda's house. At that point I knew her father was involved—everybody knew. Linda used to invite me over for dinner, but she'd tell me not to wear my earring because her father hated earrings. So I would take it out before I went to her house. Her father and I got along pretty well. We used to talk about sports. He knew I was a baseball player.

Her house was really nice. On the outside it looked like a normal house. When you went inside, it was different. It was all minted out. They had a great bar in the basement and even a little suntanning room down there, too. I loved it.

I liked to go see Linda, but I really liked it because her father trusted me. He told me he trusted me with his daughter. He gave me that opportunity to be trusted, which also was the opportunity to screw up, I guess. He basically let me stay at the house with his daughter. But when it got late, he'd say, "Okay, time to go." And I'd leave.

Greg was always very nice to me. He was a very admirable kind of guy. At the same time, though, you knew in his voice—he had a real deep voice—that you did not want to mess with this guy at all.

When I went over there for dinner, Greg would do the cooking. He cooked me these filet mignon steaks. There was actually a little grill in the kitchen, and Greg would grill steaks. There I was sitting at the table, thinking, *Wow, I have a serious Mob guy cooking for me.* He cooked them great, too. One night we even had steak and lobster. I had never even had lobster before. We had a surf-n-turf night, and it was pretty awesome.

But after that sit-down, I was forced to stay away from her and she was forced to stay away from me. Everybody knew, if you didn't abide by the rules at a sit-down, you were dead. So I was abiding by the rules. I would see Linda around the neighborhood, but I never talked to her.

About six months after the beating happened, I found out the real story. Linda wasn't the person who ratted on me to her father—it was her friend Argie. After Linda's mother called Argie's house, Argie's father demanded his daughter tell the Scarpas who she and Linda were with that night. So Argie finally told them it was me.

When I found that out, I wanted to talk to Linda, but I couldn't. Every time I saw her—she would walk by me on purpose and look at me—I had to put up this mean-guy front. I had to do it because if I gave her any indication that I wasn't pissed at her, she would approach me.

I was doing my best to keep up that "I'm pissed off at you" look for my safety, and my family's safety, as well as for her safety. Because who knew what my father was capable of? He was pretty friggin' pissed. I always gave my father a lot of credit for going over there to see Greg. I was pretty impressed with that.

Linda and I didn't talk for the next year and a half. But other things were going on in the neighborhood. Bodies were turning up here and there. As kids from the neighborhood, we knew who was doing it.

Thankfully, Stephen wasn't one of those bodies. When I saw him after the beating, I told him Greg's crew was looking for him and he should probably leave town. He was lucky they never caught up with him. If they had, he would have been history.

I used to see Linda's father driving in the neighborhood, but I wouldn't even look at him. Once, though, I was walking on Avenue I and I passed by a coffee shop just as he was coming out. He was only about fifteen feet in front of me. When I saw him, I stopped. He just turned his head and looked at me and kept walking. He didn't smile, but it wasn't an "I'm going to fucking kill you" kind of look. It was just a normal look. I looked at him, and that was it.

One day shortly after that, I was outside swinging my baseball bat on my porch. I lived right on Avenue I. Out of the corner of my eye, I saw Linda walking on the other side of the street. She looked all dressed up in a nice dress. I was wondering what the occasion was.

As I was swinging my bat, I looked up and saw her starting to walk across the street toward me. I was thinking, *Don't do it. Don't do it.* I was minding my own business, on my own porch, and she was coming over to me.

When she got close enough so I could see her, I noticed that she had matured a little bit. She was looking better than she ever did. I also noticed she was wearing a gold necklace that said *Greg and Linda* in diamonds.

"You wasted your money on that, because that'll never happen."

Those were the first words I said to her in a year and a half.

She looked at me and said, "Oh, I didn't buy it. It's my mother's."

I forgot that her mother's and father's names were Greg and Linda. I had just made a complete idiot out of myself. (Linda told me years later that she wanted me to think it was referring to me and her.)

So we talked a little bit in front of my house.

"I miss you," she said. "I'm sorry."

"I know, but we can't be seen together. We shouldn't be talking. I miss you, too, but there's nothing we can do. We can't see each other or anything."

Well, that changed in a hurry.

She left and I went inside my house, and I knew she was going to call. I knew it, so I was waiting. I wanted to answer that phone as soon as it rang. A few minutes later she did call.

"I want to see you. My sixteenth birthday is coming up in the middle of the week next week. My parents are away this weekend picking up my little brother, Joey, from sleepaway camp."

I was thinking, *Jesus, after a sit-down, her parents are away, and she's inviting me in the house. Am I that crazy to go over there?*

"I'm nervous," I told her.

"Don't worry. My friend, Justine, will be there, and her boyfriend. So there will be another couple there."

"Okay, I'll come over."

Of course, I went. We hung out the whole day and night, pretty much into the wee hours of the morning.

Linda's family moved off Avenue J in August, not long after her Sweet Sixteen, and that pretty much ended things. I saw her one time after that at the Festa di Santa Rosalia, what we called the Eighteenth

Avenue Feast. We smiled at each other, and that was it. I didn't see her again for twenty years.

When I was an adult, I always used to jog past her old house and think of her every time. One day, after I had just passed her house, I heard her voice calling me. I thought I was hearing things. I kept jogging. Then I heard her yell my name. She sounded exactly the same.

I turned around and there she was. She told me she had been in a cab going to an appointment when she saw me. She made the driver stop and let her out.

We hugged and took a walk—we always used to take walks when we were kids—and talked. We went to Coney Island. I just wanted to keep it simple and try and forget about what had happened.

I didn't want to talk about the bad things, just the good things. It was just like it was when we were kids—as if our lives hadn't been separated by twenty years. I took her up in the lighthouse at Coney Island. She was petrified of heights. So I kissed her and calmed her down.

"Why don't you come back to the house and see my mom?" she asked.

"Like your mom would want to see me? Because the last time I remember, she hated my guts."

"Everything has changed since then, and a lot of stuff has happened."

I went back to Linda's house that day. We took my car from Brooklyn to her house in Staten Island. When I walked in, her mother said, "Oh, my God." I talked to her mom for quite some time. After that day Linda and I started talking again. We still talk on the phone sometimes, and on the Internet. We're good friends. We had a good friendship when we were kids, and we still do now.

Linda has been through so much in her life. But I've always told her to "turn your wounds into wisdom." I heard Oprah Winfrey say that once.

I live in Virginia now—I'm about an hour from Baltimore and about an hour from D.C.—where I manage a restaurant.

I left Brooklyn in 1990 and went to Maryland. My friends were getting involved in gambling and drugs and a lot of them were getting killed. I had to get the hell out of there.

I saw my life going downward. I started getting involved in gambling, and the drug use had gotten worse and worse. My dad had a job offer in the D.C. area. He asked me to help the family move and then check it out. I went out there one weekend to help them, and then I went back to Brooklyn. About a month later I was on the phone with my father.

"Dad, I have to come out there. I have to get the fuck out of here because I'm dying."

That beating made me realize that if you screw around with the Mob, you're going to end up dead. I still partied, but I didn't get involved in any of that friggin' bullshit. But it really planted a seed in me. It was something that always haunted me. It never went away.

To this day I don't handle physical confrontations well, especially if there's more than one guy approaching me, and when I feel like they're going to gang up on me. I'll stay pretty much calm if it's a one-on-one encounter.

But when I feel like there are three or four guys who might try and come after me, I flip out. I'll go after them. I'm not going to stand there and take a beating. I'm going down swinging. I also don't like to be in the backseat of a car with two people, one on each side of me. I don't like that feeling of being closed in.

Through the years, though, I did hold on to some anger and hatred toward the whole situation, but it was wearing me down. You don't forget about something like that, but it did make me a better person. Sometimes a good beating will straighten you out.

If I had a chance to say something to Linda's dad right now, I would say, "Thank you." First I would thank him for not killing me, because he very easily could have. The fact that he didn't kill me gave me an opportunity to have the things that I have today. It all stemmed from that. I could've been dead, but I was spared—not too many people were spared.

I would also thank him for helping me stay away from Mob-related business. I had opportunities to get involved with other close-to-Mob things, but I stayed away. I learned a lot from that beating.

I don't get high anymore or do drugs. I've been sober since 1991, completely sober—no drinking, nothing, zero. I don't gamble at all. I don't get involved with the Mob. A lot of guys in the neighborhood always wanted to be mobsters—little guys always acting like little gangsters. I was never like that—as a matter of fact, I used to like to beat up guys like that.

So, Greg, thank you, number one, for not killing me. Number two, I learned a lot from that. I have a daughter now and she stays clear of all that kind of bullshit. She's seventeen, and a sweetheart. She's involved in softball and other sports, and she's a great girl. Thank you for giving me these opportunities.

Like I told Linda, "Turn your wounds into wisdom." My wounds have been part of a long journey. They're part of who I am today.

CHAPTER 5

J. EDGAR HOOVER, THE FBI AND MY FATHER

My father loved James Bond.

For as far back as I could remember, my brother and I used to watch 007 movies with him. We watched every single one of them—twice. I was probably nine or ten when he started telling us he was James Bond. I never really understood what he meant.

"That's your father. You don't know your father. Call me Greg, Greg Bond."

"Dad, how is that you? You're an agent? Like James Bond is a secret agent?"

Then I'd look at him and laugh. He always had such a crazy sense of humor. I just figured he was playing with us.

"Okay, Dad. You're a secret agent."

It wasn't until I was older that I learned what he

was talking about. When my father told us he was working for the FBI, my interpretation wasn't the same as other people's interpretation—that he was a rat.

I didn't fully understand what he was, but I never knew him to be a rat because he never put anybody in jail. He never took the stand and testified against anybody. So when I heard he was with the FBI, I thought he was *with* the FBI—meaning he was an agent.

I was impressed by the fact that he worked for the FBI. No wonder he used to call himself "Greg Bond." I never said to him, "Dad, oh, my God, you can't do that because you're a gangster."

I felt that my father really was above everybody else. I thought he was invincible: He was a gangster, yet he was working with the FBI. It was as if he had an edge on everyone else. I learned later that he really didn't.

My father first got involved with the FBI back in the 1960s. He was arrested on March 7, 1960, for armed robbery and released on bond. He was thirty-two at the time and a made man in the Profaci crime family, which later became the Colombo crime family. Right after that, the FBI contacted him to get information about his brother, Salvatore Scarpa, who was also a made man in the Profaci family. He told them to get lost.

In August 1961, the FBI contacted him at his Wimpy Boys Social Club because they wanted some information about a feud between two factions in the Profaci family. My father refused again. He also told them to stop contacting him because people were starting to ask questions. The FBI agents agreed, but they told him to call them if he ever wanted to talk.

On October 27, he called the New York office of the FBI and said he wanted to meet with one of the agents. He officially started working for the FBI under the Top Echelon Informant Program on November 21, 1961. But my father wasn't about to take orders from anyone—not even the FBI. He told the agents that they were not to contact him with any assignments. The agents agreed to "merely accept whatever information he desires to furnish."

There's an old saying, "While you're playing checkers, I'm playing chess." That pertained to my father. He made them think they had the upper hand, but they really didn't. He only gave them the information that he wanted them to know.

My father wasn't just a regular informant. He helped save J. Edgar Hoover's ass on three separate occasions in the '60s. During that time Hoover was getting a lot of pressure for not protecting the civil rights of African Americans in the Deep South. Hoover enlisted my father's help—first to find the killer of Medgar Evers, then to find the bodies of three murdered civil rights workers and finally to find the murderer of civil rights leader Vernon Dahmer.

The movie *Mississippi Burning* was based on the disappearance of those three civil rights workers. Although the movie indicated an African-American FBI agent, who flew down to Philadelphia, Mississippi, to question the town's mayor, broke the case, it was really my father who cracked it.

My mother went with my father to Mississippi

when he was helping Hoover find the bodies of the three civil rights workers. I've asked her to tell the story. However, as part of our research we've pieced together my father's involvement in these three civil rights cases. I'll talk about that after my mother tells you what happened.

Greg shared all his secrets with me. We were out to dinner one night when he said he had to tell me something.

"I'm working with the FBI."

"Oh, my God. Are you a rat?"

"No, I do work for them. In fact, I have to go to Mississippi and I want you to come with me."

He told me that J. Edgar Hoover wanted him to go find the bodies of three murdered civil rights workers. Hoover was getting a lot of heat because no one could find the bodies. Hoover wanted Greg to go down to Mississippi to torture one of the Klansmen to find out where the bodies were buried. An FBI agent couldn't go down there and put a gun in someone's mouth, but Greg could. The only person Hoover felt could get the job done was Greg Scarpa. I was proud of him.

I was in my late teens at the time. I told him I had never been on a plane before, but he said not to worry. He took me shopping the next day to Harpers Fashions on Kings Highway in Brooklyn. He sat in the chair while I tried on all these outfits with these big hats. He just kept telling me to get that one and that one and that one. I didn't know how many outfits I bought.

When we finally got on the plane to Mississippi, I started getting sick, but Greg was eating and drinking champagne. When that plane landed, he told me we had to take another plane. We took three planes because he wanted to be sure no one was following him to see where he was going.

When we got to the hotel, I looked up at the balcony and saw some men standing there.

I said, "Wow. Greg, look at that."

Then I saw him wink at them. They were FBI agents waiting for him to arrive. Once we were inside our room, one of the FBI agents I had already met knocked on the door. As soon as he came in, he gave Greg a gun.

"Okay, sweetheart, if I don't come back, I left you money up here [on the dresser] and a one-way ticket home."

I said okay, but I wasn't worried. He was coming back. I had so much confidence in him. I feared nothing with him. He could do anything. When he came back, he told me what had happened.

The Klansman he had to convince to talk owned a TV store. When Greg got there, he told the guy he was buying a TV and asked him to put it in his trunk. While he was doing that, Greg shoved the guy in the trunk and then drove him to an abandoned house. FBI agents followed in another car.

He tied the guy up and asked him where the bodies were. The man told him. Greg went outside to check the story with the agents, who said he was lying. Greg went back inside, put a gun in the guy's mouth and said he'd blow his brains out if he didn't tell him the truth. He did. Then Greg told the FBI agents.

When Greg came back to our room, he was all smiles. He told me they found out where the bodies were. Greg was happy that he had done it—of course, he was getting paid, too. But he was really proud of what he had accomplished. I was so happy. I just felt so safe and secure with him. Nothing was ever going to happen to Greg Scarpa.

When we got back to Brooklyn, I met the first FBI agent Greg worked with—Tony Villano. We met Tony at a restaurant in Manhattan. There we were, sitting at the table right out in the open. I told Greg I was worried that someone was going to come in and see him talking to an FBI agent. He told me not to worry about it, so I didn't worry.

That was Greg. He just did what he wanted to do. Greg didn't fear anything or anyone, especially not the FBI. One day some FBI agents came to my house. He put a movie on for some of the agents to watch in the living room while he was in the kitchen talking to one of them. The movie he put on for them: *The Godfather.* He knew what he was doing.

One time Greg, Tony and I took a ride to my sister's house in Huntington, Long Island. She had just separated from her husband. Tony was stoned out of his brain. Greg didn't like the way Tony was acting, so he coldcocked him. He knocked him out so bad that Tony was out for five minutes.

Tony quit the Bureau in 1973. Some time later, the FBI wanted to have Tony killed because he became an alcoholic and was doing all these stupid things. They were afraid he was going to say or do something that would put informants and the informant program in jeopardy. When Tony was Greg's handler, he'd go to the Flamingo Lounge, where Greg was, putting Greg in danger. Nobody there knew who Tony was, but he still wasn't supposed to do that. Greg was going to kill him for the FBI, but Tony died before he had the chance.

That was how my mother remembered what happened in Mississippi, but we've discovered the facts may be a little different. What's interesting, though, is the information about my father buying a television set from a suspect who owned or managed an appliance store appeared in each and every story.

However, the account from my father's first FBI handler, Tony Villano, the agent my mother mentioned, was written in the late 1970s. That seemed to be where the story about the TV first surfaced, leading us to believe that somehow that story was incorporated in the telling—and continued retelling—of my father's subsequent work in Mississippi. Either that, or maybe more than one of the three suspects— or even all three—really did sell televisions.

In 1977, Villano wrote a book, *Brick Agent: Inside the Mafia for the FBI,* about his years in the FBI working with Mafia informants. (During Hoover's time, a street agent for the FBI was said to be "on the bricks.") Two of the people in the book, who were identified with pseudonyms, were actually my father.

In his book Villano talked about the first time my father had a falling-out with the FBI, which was before the two ever met. Apparently, my father believed that the Bureau owed him $1,500 for the work he did for them in Mississippi.

After Villano found my father's name in the FBI's filed on closed informants, he got him the money he was owed. However, he wasn't able to get my father to cooperate with him. So he challenged my father, who he said was built like "an ox of a man," to an arm-wrestling contest. The fact that they wrestled to a draw impressed my father, who decided to "make a marriage" with Villano, as the agent called it.

Villano thought of my father as "a friend," and he bent—as well as broke—the law to help him. He even used my father as his bookie to make illegal sports bets for him. One time a criminal who could have implicated my father in some robberies offered to cooperate with the FBI. Villano got the man to back off by making up a story that the Colombo family planned to kidnap his daughter if he talked. That guy died in prison.

In his book Villano said that all the time he worked with my father, he had to reassure himself that their relationship wasn't "the ultimate perversion of the whole law-enforcement idea. In my mind, what we did was justified on the grounds of the greatest good."

But other FBI agents didn't agree. "I had a discussion with Tony that made me think that Scarpa thought he had a license to kill," a retired agent recalled. "Around 1970, an informant for the Drug Enforcement Administration got blown away, and the DEA heard that Scarpa was the triggerman. They wanted to interrogate Scarpa, and Tony did a tap dance to obstruct their investigation. Scarpa was not arrested or charged with that murder."

In his book Villano credited my father with finding out the name of the man who executed Medgar Evers, the Mississippi field secretary for the NAACP. Evers was shot in the back by a rifle bullet in the driveway of his Jackson home on June 12, 1963.

Villano said the FBI contacted my father, whom he referred to as "Julio," to go down to Mississippi to "persuade" a member of the white Citizens' Council to give up the name of the person who assassinated Evers. The FBI, in return, paid my father for his services, as well as guaranteed him a walk on an armed-robbery charge he was facing.

"If he would assist the investigation in Mississippi, he would be the beneficiary of the best the bureau could do for him," Villano wrote in his book.

Villano said my father agreed, so my father and his girlfriend flew to Miami Beach to establish an alibi. He checked her into a hotel and then went to Jackson, Mississippi, to a store managed by the white Citizens' Council member. My father told the guy he had just moved to Jackson from Chicago and needed to buy a television set. After the purchase he told the man to hold it and he would return later that night—although he might be a little late.

Around 9:20 P. M., my father showed back up at the store and asked the manager, who was alone, to put the television in his car. He said he had a bad back and couldn't lift anything. The manager agreed. When they got to the car, my father told him to put the TV in the backseat because the trunk was filled with clothes.

When he opened the door and leaned in to secure the television, my father pushed him to the floor and jumped onto the backseat. Then he shoved a gun in the manager's ribs and ordered him to stay put and not open his mouth. An FBI agent, who had been lying on the front seat, jumped up and started driving.

Villano said they drove south for a few hours, with a car full of agents following them. Finally they arrived at a deserted building somewhere in the Louisiana bayou. The agents surrounded the house, while my father brought the guy inside. He tied him to a chair near an open window. My father told the man he worked for the grand dragon of the Chicago chapter of the Ku Klux Klan, who was unhappy with the assassination of Medgar Evers because he hadn't coordinated it.

My father told the appliance store manager to tell him who did it and he would let him go. The guy spilled his guts. My father then went outside to talk to the agents, who had heard everything through the open window. They said the guy's story was a crock—the names weren't right and the facts didn't match up with their information.

According to Villano, my father threatened the guy, but he lied again. For the third time my father asked the man to tell him what he wanted to know. But that time he wasn't taking any chances. He stuck his gun in the guy's mouth and said if he didn't tell him the absolute truth, he was going to blow his head off, which he said later he would have done.

It worked. Villano said my father told the guy to

tell him the story again—slowly—so he could write it down. When my father finished writing the man's statement, he told him to sign it. In the end, because of my father's involvement, the FBI arrested Byron De La Beckwith for the murder of Medgar Evers.

Although Hoover's office tried to say Beckwith was tracked down by other means—his fingerprints were allegedly found on the rifle—Villano said that was "pure hokum." Two all-white juries ultimately couldn't reach verdicts in the case in 1964. But finally Beckwith was convicted of the murder in 1994, dying in prison in 2001 at age eighty.

In his book Villano said after he confirmed the story with my father, he "was ashamed that the people I worked for had to go outside the bureau to find someone to perform their dirty work."

The second time Hoover and the FBI needed my father's help was to find the bodies of the three murdered civil rights workers—twenty-one-year-old African-American James Chaney from Mississippi and two white men from New York, Andrew Goodman, twenty, and Michael Schwerner, twenty-four—in Philadelphia, Mississippi. That was the case that my mother remembered.

This story was strikingly similar to the Medgar Evers story. The suspect, a member of the Ku Klux Klan, owned an appliance store. My father bought a TV, went back to pick it up late at night, kidnapped the guy, took him to an undisclosed location, put a gun in his mouth and demanded to know where the bodies were. The guy lied at first; then he finally told the truth.

The FBI recovered the bodies, thanks to my

father. After a mistrial in 1967, Edgar Ray Killen, who was thought to be the ringleader, was again charged with three counts of murder on January 7, 2005, forty-one years after the crime. He was convicted of manslaughter in the deaths of the three civil rights workers in June of that year.

The third time Hoover and the FBI sought out my father's help during the civil rights era was in 1966 when they asked him to find out who had firebombed Vernon Dahmer's house in Forrest County, Mississippi on January 10, 1966. Dahmer was an African-American farmer and merchant who had agreed to make his grocery store available as a place for African Americans to pay poll taxes.

Dahmer's wife and ten-year-old daughter were also badly burned in the fire, which had been set by Ku Klux Klansmen. "On January 21st, the Jackson, Mississippi office of the FBI called the New York office and, as recorded in an internal memo, requested the use of informant NY-3461—Gregory Scarpa—for a special assignment."

Klansman Lawrence Byrd, the owner of Byrd's Radio & TV Service in Laurel, Mississippi, was a suspect in the case. Again, as in the other stories, my father went to the shop around nine at night to buy a television just as Byrd was about to close up. My father asked Byrd to put the TV in the car because he had a bad back. Then he and an FBI agent kidnapped Byrd and drove him to a barracks at Camp Shelby, a military base in the Mississippi swampland. My father beat the crap and a confession out of Byrd, who was ultimately sentenced to ten years for arson.

In 2007—after extensive research—Judge W.O. "Chet" Dillard, a former Mississippi district attorney, published the book *The Final Curtain: Burning Mississippi by the FBI*. The book was written to expose FBI tampering in civil rights cases in Mississippi.

In his book onetime DA Dillard said, "The records prove beyond a doubt that JEH (J. Edgar Hoover) sent Scarpa into Mississippi [on] three different cases. The treatment of a key man or men were [*sic*] all the same. Kidnapping, torture and extortion to get what they wanted. They are the same story, only the names are changed."

My father had a falling-out with the bureau in 1975 and stopped providing information to the feds. But in 1980, Special Agent R. Lindley "Lin" DeVecchio wanted my father back. And he got him. A highly decorated FBI agent, Lin DeVecchio became my father's handler. "Mr. Delo" was Lin's code name when he telephoned my father.

My mother can tell you more about Lin DeVecchio.

When Greg decided to meet with Lin, we were living on Fifty-Fifth Street. Greg didn't want Lin coming down that block because it was a dead end. He was afraid that if anyone came to the house when Lin was there, there wouldn't be a way for him to get out.

So the first time I met Lin—I already knew that he was an FBI agent because Greg told me that he was going to meet with him—I had taken a ride with Greg to Twentieth Avenue or somewhere around there. Lin was in a car, and Greg parked behind him. Lin got out of the car and sat in the back of our car, and that's when Greg introduced me to him. Then Greg and Lin got out of our car and went back to Lin's car.

I saw Lin more when we moved to Avenue J and East Third Street, which wasn't a dead-end street. Lin used to come by in the morning. Every time Lin came over, he'd sit in the kitchen. I remember one time when he came to the house, I was going to go upstairs so they could talk. But Greg said, "No, sit down, sweetheart. Don't worry about it." So I always sat with them.

Greg and Lin were very close. Lin idolized Greg. When Greg talked, Lin would just look at him. Lin even admitted he and Greg had a friendship. Lin came by the house every week and Greg would give him money in exchange for the addresses and phone numbers of his loan-sharking customers who owed him money.

I was there when Lin gave Greg this note with all the names of the guys who were going to get arrested by the Drug Enforcement Administration on drug charges. It was 1987. Greg Junior was on the list, so Greg sent Gregory away on the lam to Florida because Lin told him that if Gregory was going to stand trial, it would be better if he went on trial alone.

So that's what happened. Lin knew where Gregory was hiding. Greg Junior was arrested ten months later, after he was featured on *America's Most Wanted*. He was tried separately and convicted in 1988. He was sentenced to twenty years in federal prison for racketeering and extortion involving cocaine and marijuana distribution.

I knew Greg was living a double life, but I never really thought that anything could happen to him because he had everything under control. He had the gangsters under control; he had the FBI under control. I didn't fear anything. I never thought the gangsters were going to kill him, because Greg was too smart for them. He was manipulating everybody.

Lin wanted to be a gangster. He was an FBI agent, but he loved the fact that my father had these feelings for him, which he did. My father cared for him. When my father cared for somebody, he went all out for you, but he still wasn't going to sell himself out.

Even though he cared for Lin, he still knew what he was doing and it was going to benefit him, not Lin. But Lin was playing both ends because he wanted to be a part of the scene, but he was doing it from the FBI side. There were strong feelings there on a friend-ship level—my father cared for him and he cared for my father. He really did.

CHAPTER 6

THE GRIM REAPER

My father was one of the most feared hit men in the New York Mafia. An enforcer in the Colombo crime family, he was known as "the Grim Reaper" because if you did wrong and you were in the life, or you hurt his family or anyone he cared about, it was his job to bring you death. He'd kill you.

Most mobsters were discreet around their families, but not my father. He started to bring the outside world home with him. My father didn't make any attempt to hide his third family—the Colombo crime family—from our family. Mobsters came over to the house all the time. They'd discuss Mob business in front of Joey and me. My brother and I didn't want to hear about those things because we were still so young.

Sometimes my father's friends would disappear—people I knew and loved. I asked questions about them and he would say they had passed away. I figured out that they must have been killed, but I didn't want to believe that my father had anything to do with their murders.

I really started to figure things out when I was in my midteens. It wasn't all that much of a shock to me because I had grown up in that lifestyle with all my father's friends. Even though I didn't know to what extent he was involved, I had been around it all my life. So it didn't affect me the way people might have thought.

Once I did realize what was happening, my father was honest about what he did. Of course, I was worried, but he had a way about him that made me believe that he was invincible and that nobody could ever touch him. Looking back, I guess that was an immature way of thinking, but I was only a kid.

My father was such a strong person that I believed in my heart that he would overcome any obstacle that came his way. I felt that anybody who tried to interfere with him would be the one to get hurt, not him.

When my father started to bring Mob business into the house, it really affected my brother and me. He would talk to my mother in front of us. He didn't hide anything just because we were in the room. We didn't want to hear about someone being murdered or missing, but it was just regular conversation in our house.

I started hearing things when I was around fifteen or sixteen. I was old enough to understand what was going on at that point. And for a while I had a lot of anger toward my father, since I loved some of the people who were disappearing.

I started blaming my father for a lot of things that were happening. Although I didn't really have too much knowledge as to who else was involved, I was just blaming him. At the time I was very disturbed about all of it, and I let him know. He was pretty much ignoring it—there was nothing he could really say. My brother and I just had to deal with what was happening. We had no say in anything.

Growing up, I never thought there was a code of honor in the Mob—even though there was supposed to be—because I knew that people were disappearing in their own crime families. If you did something wrong, even though you were in the same family, you were getting killed. There was never any honor.

One of the people I remember hearing about that my father killed was Mary Bari. It was 1984. Mary had been dating Colombo consigliere Alphonse "Allie Boy" Persico, who had gone into hiding in the 1980s rather than face twenty years for extortion. My mother said Lin DeVecchio told him that Mary Bari was an informant who was a problem and had to be taken care of before she gave up Allie Boy.

So Mary was lured to my father's Wimpy Boys Social Club on the pretense that she was being offered a job as a cocktail waitress. Instead, she was met by my father and some of his crew, thrown to the ground, and shot in the head by my father.

A couple days after the murder, Annie Sessa, the wife of Colombo consigliere Carmine Sessa, came to the house to see my mother. They were talking in front of me.

"Can you believe the dog found Mary Bari's ear?"

My mother looked like she was going to throw up. Annie was smirking.

"What dog? What ear?" I wanted to know what

was going on, but they didn't say any more about it. My mother knew about the murder, but she didn't know anything about Mary Bari's ear being shot off.

We found out later it was a sick joke. There was no dog and Mary didn't lose her ear. Annie was making this joke in front of me—telling my mother because she thought it was entertaining. My mother didn't find the joke amusing.

Soon my father's murders got closer to home. When I found out that Joe Brewster had been killed, I was inconsolable. That was devastating to me. I loved him. Joe Brewster had a personality above and beyond personalities, a smile beyond smiles. And for Joe Brewster to get killed by my father? How could he do that? It was unbelievable. He was my father's right-hand man. Joe and my father were so close that my father had been the best man at his wedding and was godfather to Joe's son.

My mother said that Lin told my father, "You know we got to take care of this guy before he starts talking." My father told Lin not to worry about it, he'd take care of it.

At that point in my life I knew my father was killing people, but I turned away from it. It was almost as if I had taken an oath to my family. I knew what my father was doing, but he was my father. There was nothing I could do about it. I just had to turn the other cheek. I had to try to block it out and not ask too many questions because I really didn't want to know, especially about people that I cared about.

One of the reasons my father had Joe Brewster

killed was because he was drinking pretty heavily. He was always coming to the house drunk. I remember one day I asked him to sign my yearbook. When I looked at his signature, it was just a bunch of scribbles. He couldn't write because he was so smashed.

But the main reason was because Joe had become a born-again Christian and didn't want to be in the life anymore. My father agreed with Lin that Joe had to go because he knew too much. And my father said he couldn't trust him anymore.

I remember my parents saying that Joe Brewster was gone. I asked what happened to him. They told me he was sick and had passed away. They lied to me. When I found out that he had been murdered, I stayed in my room, in the dark, crying. I loved Joe Brewster. He was so close to us.

I didn't ask my father if he had killed him, although I had an idea. I had to keep telling myself that he was murdered, but my father didn't do it. Maybe Carmine did it, or maybe Mario did it, or maybe some other member of my father's crew did it. But in my mind there was no way my father did it. That was my defense mechanism toward him killing people. I reasoned that he might've known about it, but he didn't do it. I might've been wrong, which I was, but that was how I protected my sanity.

Of course, it bothered me that he condoned these murders. But as the daughter of somebody who killed people, I had to learn just to block things out. I didn't want to believe that my father could be capable of killing people. I knew that he could and I knew that he did, but I had to turn my mind off to it. I had to preoccupy myself with other things.

When I finally accepted the truth, I couldn't understand how my father could have murdered Joe. I didn't understand how they could kill their own friends. I was—and still am—tormented by it.

One of the murders he planned devastated my brother. My mother can tell the story.

Joey worshiped Greg. But while he wanted to be like Greg, he still wanted to be his own person. Of course, Greg wanted Joey to do things his way. He didn't like the clothes Joey wore and didn't like his haircut. He also didn't like Joey's friends. He wanted Joey to hang out with his crew. Joey, of course, wanted to be with his own friends—kids his age who liked doing the same things he did.

Joey's best friend was Patrick Porco. They were as close as brothers. Patrick used to sleep over at the house all the time. Patrick was like another son to Greg and me.

When Patrick and Joey were about seventeen, they started buying small amounts of marijuana and cocaine and selling it to other kids in the neighborhood. I knew about the pot, but not about the cocaine. I found out later that Greg knew about the cocaine. He didn't want me to worry, so he didn't tell me.

Greg was always worried about Joey. He was afraid that Joey would get killed. When Joey was out, Greg couldn't sleep until he came home—it didn't matter how late it was. He'd keep looking out the window or else he would lie in bed with his eyes open until he heard Joey's car pull up.

One day I was cleaning Joey's room and I decided to turn over his mattress. I couldn't believe what I found—hundreds of $20 packets of cocaine. I started screaming. I yelled for Greg to come upstairs to show him what I found. When Greg saw the cocaine, he lied to me. He told me Joey was just keeping it for a friend.

On the night of Halloween, 1989, Joey and Patrick got into an argument with a neighborhood kid named Dominick Masseria. Later that night Joey and Patrick and two of their friends, Reyes Aviles and Craig Sobel, got into Aviles's white limo and went looking to settle the beef. Someone in Aviles's car fired a sawed-off shotgun and killed Masseria, who was also seventeen. He was standing on the steps of Our Lady of Guadalupe Church in Bensonhurst.

Greg was frantic when he heard about what had happened. He was scared for Joey and Patrick. To keep them safe, Greg sent the boys to his farm in New Jersey to stay with his older son Frank and his family.

Aviles surrendered to police on November 7. Still, Joey and Patrick only stayed in New Jersey for several weeks. They were bored and homesick so they went back to Brooklyn. Soon the police were involved. Then they started leaning on Patrick to get him to talk about who else was involved.

During the investigation into Dominick Masseria's murder, Lin DeVecchio called Greg at the house. Usually, Greg and Lin talked openly on the phone, but this time Lin told Greg to go to an outside telephone and call him back. So Greg and I left the house and drove to a nearby pay phone. I waited in the car while Greg talked to Lin.

When Greg got back in the car, he was really upset. Greg said Lin told him that Patrick was going to rat on Joey about Masseria's murder. Greg didn't say much on the way back home. All he said was that he was trying to figure out how to kill Patrick.

Greg wanted Joseph "Joe Fish" Marra to do the actual shooting, but he needed Joey to get Patrick to the meeting. When Greg told Joey, Joey tried to talk Greg out of killing Patrick. He told Greg there was no way his best friend would rat on him. But Greg wasn't going to change his mind. He told Joey he knew what was best and Patrick had to be killed.

But on his way to the house, Joe Fish's car broke down and he was stuck on the other side of town. So Greg told Joey he'd have to kill Patrick himself. Joey had no choice. He had to do what he was told.

Joey left the house with his cousin. It was May 27, 1990. When he came back a few hours later, he was alone. He went right up to his room. Greg told me that Patrick had been murdered. I went upstairs to comfort Joey. He was on the floor in a fetal position, crying. I got down on the floor with him and held him. He told me he couldn't do the murder, so his cousin killed Patrick.

Greg wanted Joey and me to go to Patrick's wake. He didn't want anything to look suspicious. Joey certainly would have gone if Patrick had died any other way, but Joey refused to go. He was too upset and depressed, so I went alone.

When Carol, Patrick's mother, spotted me, she started crying hysterically. Then I started crying. I told her Joey couldn't come because he was too upset.

I've often thought about the people my father murdered and the families that he destroyed, and it's very painful and disturbing. I knew what that felt like because my brother was murdered, too.

In the life you never get to say good-bye to the people you love. People just disappear. One day they're there and the next day they're gone.

CHAPTER 7

DADDY'S LITTLE GIRL

I was always daddy's little girl.

At my Sweet Sixteen I had him light the sixteenth candle on my birthday cake. The sixteenth candle is supposed to be for your boyfriend. I had a boyfriend, but I wasn't going to have him light my sixteenth candle. My sixteenth candle was for my father.

I had the DJ say, "For the true love of Linda's life, Daddy." Then the DJ played the song "Daddy's Little Girl." My father was just beaming when the DJ called him up. He was so happy and there was so much love in his eyes. I still cry when I watch that video.

It was a really great party, too—held at La Mer in Brooklyn—except for the fact that not many of my friends showed up. They were scared away by my father's reputation. I had given invitations to a lot of the kids in school—guys and girls—and they all said they were coming. But although all the boys came, only a few girls attended. My friends Justine and Melissa were there.

But there was a whole table that was empty that was supposed to be for the other girls. I felt terrible that they didn't come, like any kid would feel if people didn't show up to her party. My parents asked me where they all were. All I could say was that they probably weren't coming. I was embarrassed. My father told me not to worry about it and just to have fun. He said the people who came were my real friends, but I still felt bad.

None of those girls ever told me why they didn't come. I just stopped talking to them after that because it was apparent that they weren't really my friends. Although I was a loner in a lot of ways, I was still always trying to fit in.

But there were a lot of made men and family there to help me celebrate. My Sweet Sixteen was beautiful. I had a Madonna look-alike there, a Michael Jackson look-alike and break-dancers. They did shows. I had these big, really cute dolls with balloons on them propped on the tables. Guests could take those dolls home. It was a very extravagant party.

Growing up, I was spoiled somewhat. My father didn't always give us everything we wanted, but we did have a lot. We definitely had more things than other kids had. We had the nicest cars and the nicest clothes.

I got my first fur coat when I was six. It was a rabbit coat, but I felt funny wearing it because none of my friends had anything like that. I told my mother that I didn't really like it. Of course, she said it was beautiful.

"But it's a rabbit. Did they really kill a rabbit?" I asked.

I was a kid and I was really confused about the rabbit thing; nobody else had anything like it. I was six, wearing a fur coat and diamond stud earrings.

I loved my father so much. I used to love looking at him, just his presence in the room, and listening to his voice. He had a deep voice. Singer Barry White was big in those days and my dad's voice sounded just like his. Sometimes when Barry White's songs would come on the radio, my father would start singing and tell us that was him on the radio.

He sounded so much like Barry White that when he used to imitate him in front of us, my brother and I would look at each other and then ask, "Is that really you?" We didn't know for sure, especially when he sang "You're the First, the Last, My Everything." He would do his voice exactly.

One day I was watching him as he sat at the kitchen table, talking to my mother, my aunt and a couple of his friends. I thought, *God, what would I do without my father?*

I always wanted to be around him, to be with him. If I was sitting next to him, I'd be almost on top of him. Our feet would even be together. He'd beg me to give him some room, but he loved having me with him.

"Look at our feet. We got the same feet. You got the same feet as me," he'd tell me.

That's how close we were. That's the kind of relationship that we had. My mother used to ask why I never sat next to her. It's not that I didn't love my mother, but I was completely a daddy's girl. Joey, though, was totally a mama's boy.

My father had this very, very soft side, especially when it came to me. I was his baby girl. He was so affectionate and loving. I was his little girl, and that was it. As I got older, I sometimes took advantage of that.

When we moved to Eighty-Second Street, I was still in high school, and I really didn't have any girl-friends. My friends growing up my whole life were always guys, even until this day. I hung out with a lot of kids—girls and boys—but the girls weren't really my friends.

Not long after we moved, I met these twin girls, Nicole and Teresa. They were friends with every-body, but they hated me.

Nicole and Teresa were snotty little rich girls like me, but their father wasn't a made guy. He was a regular working guy. They didn't have the crowd around them that I had, but they hung out with the same type of people that I did. Teresa was going out with Carmine Sessa's son. They liked the same scenery as I did at the time. They wanted to hang out with all the street guys.

Carmine's wife, Annie, was at the house one day and she talked to me about them.

"You should make friends with Nicole and Teresa."

I wasn't having any part of it.

"I'm not making friends with them. They're so snotty."

"Well, I'm going to talk to them and see if they want to talk to you."

They didn't. They said the same things about me that I said about them. They told Annie they didn't want to be friends with me because I was such a snob.

The funny thing was, I wasn't a snob. I honestly never knew why nobody wanted to talk to me. I didn't really understand it. Even though my father told me when I was younger that it was because of who he was, I didn't think much about what he was saying.

Maybe I had this persona of being a show-off, when I really didn't realize that I was. I never thought I was a show-off. It was instilled in me by the age of six that having nice things was okay. But I never was the type to stick it in people's faces, like some of the girls I knew.

They had everything—I even felt like they had more than me—and they *really* showed it off. I was never like that. But everybody loved them, so I never understood why people liked them, but they didn't like me.

Recently I ran into a guy who's a friend of mine— a single dad—at my kids' school, who kind of put things into perspective for me. He told me that when he's talking to other women in the schoolyard and I go near him, they walk away. I was shocked.

"Are you serious?" I didn't realize that. "Why?"

"I don't know. It doesn't really matter."

"I really want an answer. Are you joking around with me?"

"No, I'm serious. Take notice the next time there's a group of mothers I'm talking to. Whenever you come over to me, you'll notice they walk away."

"Why do you think that is?"

"Well, Linda, when you walk into the schoolyard, you have a presence about you, an attitude."

"I have an attitude?"

"I don't even think you realize it."

"I don't realize it, because I *don't* have an attitude."

"Linda, I know you, but people who don't know you, they would think that you do."

"Why?"

"I don't know. It's just the way you look."

The more I thought about it, I realized it was because I was always on the defensive, thinking that somebody had something to say to me about my father, or the life, or whatever. That's basically why I became so disliked. I was always on the defensive, and I've always been on the defensive.

But growing up not understanding why people didn't want to talk made me very insecure. It made me not want to be sociable with anyone. People thought I didn't want to be bothered. It wasn't that I was snobby. Instead, I was just going into a shell. I didn't know how to socialize because people weren't talking to me. If I was just being me, and no one wanted to talk to me, then I figured I must be doing something wrong. I thought they just didn't like me, but I didn't know why.

Despite the fact that Nicole, Teresa and I didn't want anything to do with each other, Annie wasn't giving up. For some reason, she wanted me to make friends with them. So she planned this date for us to meet. She set it up so I would have to go to their house.

The minute I got there, I was miserable. We were

in their room and they were playing with makeup. One of their friends was there and they were putting makeup on her. I felt like I was in hell.

Then they decided to put makeup on me. I tried to get out of it, but it didn't work. They started doing my makeup. They told me I had really nice eyes and the makeup looked pretty. I started thinking maybe they weren't so bad, after all. That's when we started to become friends. We used to joke about how we were forced to become friends.

We actually became best friends. We started out hating each other and ended up loving each other. In my entire life they were probably the only friends that I ever really considered my best friends.

One day their mother let me drive her car because I had a license and they only had learner's permits. I wound up smashing the car on one side. Their mother was really pissed, and she wanted to know who was going to pay to get it fixed.

One of my father's friends owned a body shop. So I brought the car there and told him he had to fix it. He wanted to know who was going to pay for it. I told him nobody, but he'd better fix that car. The guy fixed the car—and I didn't get in any trouble when my father found out.

Like me, most of the kids I knew had nice cars—Cadillacs, Lincolns, Grand Prix and Monte Carlos. I drove a Mercedes. Everybody had done-up cars. They had spokes on the wheels and radios in their cars with big speakers, along with the fuzzy dice and air fresheners hanging from the rearview mirrors. In the summer everybody was always getting their cars washed and waxed.

A big thing about Brooklyn when I was growing up was Eighty-Sixth Street—the main east-west street in Bensonhurst. It was mobbed with guys and girls hanging out in the street, sitting next to their cars on lounge chairs or on the trunks or the hoods of their cars, listening to their radios. It was like the beach on the street. The street was so long that it took us two hours to get from one end to the other because we stopped here and there to talk to various guys. It was insane.

If you had a convertible, which I had at one point, you drove around with the top down even in the middle of the winter. It didn't matter. People even got dressed up to go to Eighty-Sixth Street and hang out. In the summer the girls wore heels and they all had these poufy hairdos and long nails. The guys wore wife-beater T-shirts and gold chains with the horns and crosses on them around their necks. The boys grew their hair kind of long, and most of them styled it in a DA, which stood for "duck's ass."

That was Brooklyn in the '80s—showing off your car, driving in your car, hanging out in your car. That was a big deal.

I was seventeen when I started going to clubs— younger than I should have been. There were clubs for kids around seventeen or a little older everywhere in Brooklyn when I was growing up, and these were all owned by Mob guys.

Nicole, Teresa and I went out every night. We had a routine for every day of the week. Wednesdays was Pastels; Strings was Thursdays. On Friday night we went to the Bay Club. Every night it was a different hot spot. We'd get dressed up and go out and have a good time. I still did okay in school, so everything was fine with my parents.

There were a lot of after-hours clubs, but I never went to those because there was always trouble, and my father never wanted me in them. My after-hours hangout was the Vegas Diner. My friends and I would go out to Pastels or wherever; and then at 4 or 4:30 A.M. when they shut the doors, we'd be at the diner. It was always jam-packed. That was a big hot spot, too.

My father allowed me to go to the regular clubs, but I had to go to the clubs where his friends were, so they could keep an eye on me. They didn't like that, though, because if anything happened to me, they'd have to answer to my father. I didn't like it, either. So I'd leave with my friends, and not let his friends know I left—and that would drive everybody a little bit crazy.

I'd tell the valet that a particular car—whichever one I happened to like—that belonged to one of my father's friends was mine, even though it wasn't. I'd take the car and we'd go out all night and have a good time with my friends. Then I'd go home and park it in the driveway. The next morning my father would see the car.

"Linda, whose car is in the driveway?"

I'd tell him whose car it was.

"How did it get there?"

"Well, I borrowed it."

Then later he'd get a phone call.

"Your daughter took my car."

He'd just say, "Linda, you shouldn't do that. You can't just take someone's car."

I really didn't get in trouble. He just told me not to do it again, but I still did it every time.

Even though I did some crazy shit when I was a teenager, I still didn't get in trouble with my father.

It was kind of strange, though, that my parents didn't mind me going out so much. Nobody said anything about it, so I just did it. Whenever we went to a club, there would be a line around the block. There was no line for us, though. I would go right up to the door, tell them who I was and they'd let us right in.

Even though I didn't like my father's friends watching out for me, I always felt protected. I received a certain respect that other people didn't get, so no one really got out of line with me. If anybody ever tried anything, one of my father's friends would say, "Oh, watch out! That's Greg's daughter." And the person would back off. But there were some people who wouldn't back off and they'd get a beating. I never liked that. I always tried to stay away from that part of it because I didn't want anybody to get hurt.

But there were times that I took advantage of who I was.

One night I left a club alone. I got in my car to drive home. This guy left at the same time and started following me. I didn't know who he was. I wanted to go home, but I wasn't going to let this guy follow me and find out where I lived.

So instead of going to my house, I made him follow me to my father's social club. I pulled up in front of the club, and he pulled up right behind me. He saw all the guys hanging out, but he didn't realize who they were. Greg Junior was standing outside. He came over to my car.

"What's up, dollface?"

"This guy is following me everywhere, and I just want to go home."

When Gregory got mad, you could see the horns coming out of his head.

"What do you mean, he's following you?"

"He's followed me for like a half hour, Greg. I want to go home."

Gregory went right over to the guy's car and knocked on the window. The guy opened the window. Gregory picked him up by his shirt and pulled his head through the window. He gave him one shot and knocked the guy out.

"All right, Lin, go ahead. Go home. I got it from here."

"Okay, thanks, see you later."

I didn't like people getting hurt because of me. Yet, this guy was annoying me, so what did I do? I turned to Greg. I didn't think he was going do that, but he did.

When I graduated from high school, my father asked me what I wanted to do. I said I wanted to go to our condo in Singer Island in Florida for a week.

But a week turned into five months. I loved living there. Singer Island was gorgeous. It was so different from my life in Brooklyn. My father was sending me money to live on. I was going out to clubs with some girls I met there. I was happy and having fun.

The condo was beautiful. It was right on the water. I could go out on the terrace and look at the ocean and the pristine white sand. I had a Chrysler LeBaron convertible and I'd drive along the coastline, with the top down, listening to a tape of Laura Branigan singing "Self Control."

And I met a guy. He had curly blond hair and blue eyes. His name was Rob. If he lived in Brooklyn, his name would have been Robert. He was beautiful and so different from the guys I knew growing up. He was a beach bum. He had been adopted and his parents were taking care of him. I was spending most of my time with him. It was the best time of my life.

Being in Florida was a totally different lifestyle. The people were different; the way of life was so different. It was calm, not like city life. And I was free from everything that caused me pain. Sometimes Rob and I would fall asleep on the terrace and wake up in the morning to the cool breeze of the ocean. It was so peaceful. I was so happy. Maybe too happy.

But my dad was not happy that I was alone in Florida with a guy. But most of all he wasn't happy because I was far away from him. He missed me and wanted me to come home. I told him I was happy and I wasn't going to leave. He threatened to cut me off. No more money. He figured I'd have no choice but to go home. I got a job pumping gas. I didn't care. For the first time I was at peace.

My father wouldn't give up. He sent my mother to Florida to bring me home. I hated them. I cried as the plane took off. I watched everything I loved at that moment—the sparkling blue ocean, the white sandy beaches, the palm trees, my beautiful life—fade into the distance.

I hated going back. I looked out as the plane descended into the city. Everything was cold and gray and lifeless. That was the crossroads of my life. I was going to make them pay for bringing me back against my will. It wasn't long before I met a guy, got married and got pregnant.

CHAPTER 8

BLOOD BROTHERS

In August 1986, my father developed bleeding ulcers from years of taking aspirin for a back injury. He was admitted to Victory Memorial Hospital in Brooklyn. The medication couldn't stop the bleeding and the doctors told him he'd need a transfusion.

My mother can tell the story.

We were living on Eighty-Second Street. Greg came home one night and said, "You know, Lin, I don't feel so good. I feel very dizzy and sick."

I called the doctor and then I took him to the office. The doctor said that he had to go in the hospital because he was bleeding internally. Greg told me to take him to Victory Memorial Hospital because it was on Eighty-Sixth Street and close to the house. He didn't want me to have to travel too far if they kept him.

While we were there, I tried to help him get up out of bed to go to the bathroom. He just, like, collapsed in my arms. Blood was coming out all over. I was screaming. They had to call a doctor to do emergency surgery.

The doctor explained that he needed a lot of blood. I called my doctor and he told me to get the blood from people I knew. The nurse at the hospital told me the same thing. I called Larry and he got all the guys from Greg's club to come down, as well as some of our family. There were thirty people who gave their blood for Greg. Six out of the thirty were Greg's blood type.

There was a rumor going around that Greg called on his friends and family to give him blood because he didn't want to take the chance of getting blood from African Americans because he was prejudiced. That was just not true. Greg was pretty much going in and out of consciousness. He didn't even know what was going on. I was making all the decisions for him.

Because of the AIDS virus, the hospital and the doctors advised me to call family and friends first. The medical people didn't know much about HIV at that time, but they thought it affected more African Americans, which was probably where that rumor started.

However, the hospital gave him the blood without testing it for HIV. One of the donors—Paul Mele, a weight lifter who was in Greg's crew—had contracted the virus, apparently from a dirty steroid needle. Paul died six months after donating his blood. Greg got AIDS from that blood.

I went to the hospital and saw that Greg didn't look good. It was about six o'clock in the morning. He was in the ICU and the doctor was standing over him. Greg had tubes in his nose and blood was coming out. They had him on an ice bed because he had a fever. I asked the doctor what was going on, but he told me Greg was doing good.

I got in touch with Gregory, Greg's son. Then Scappy called the hospital and told me to "get him out of there." So I called my doctor and told him Greg was getting worse. We got a private ambulance to transfer him to Mount Sinai in Manhattan. He had three major surgeries—every other day was a surgery. They took out his stomach—we didn't know he had AIDS yet—and the doctor made a stomach for him out of his intestines. He was in the ICU at Mount Sinai for nearly three months.

Lin DeVecchio even visited Greg when he was in the hospital. One time Lin was in the room and I had gone downstairs for something. I was coming back up in the elevator and two Mafia bosses got on. They were going to see Greg. I didn't know what to say, but I knew they couldn't go up there with Lin in the room. I told them that Greg was really bad that day and they couldn't visit him. So they left.

When my father was first in Mount Sinai, he kept getting a number of infections. The doctors didn't know where these infections were coming from, since they didn't know he had AIDS.

In the beginning he wasn't conscious, and it was very hard for me to see him like that. I started going through a very bad phase, smoking a lot of pot just to escape from the world. I was getting high, trying to take away my pain somehow. I wasn't able to deal with the real world at all.

One day my mother came home from visiting my father and asked if I wanted to go to the hospital. She said the doctors didn't know if my father was going to make it through the night. So I went to see him with my mother.

When I got to his room, I saw him just lying there. I leaned over him and hugged him.

"Daddy, please don't leave me, please. Open your eyes, Dad, please. Talk to me. Don't leave."

I was crying hysterically. My tears were flowing onto his face. Then for a split second he opened his eyes and spoke.

"I'm not going anywhere."

My mother was in total shock. She called the nurses and doctors in to tell them that he spoke. I was so happy that he said that to me. And I believed him. I believed that he wasn't going anywhere.

He came to shortly after that and we knew that he was going to make it. A couple days later I went to see him and he was sitting up. He was very swollen everywhere. I tried to rub his ankles and his legs, but he asked me to stop because it hurt.

I was just so relieved. My father had been on his deathbed, but I felt that he heard me, and he didn't leave after that. But he was living out a death sentence, anyway.

It wasn't long before the doctors found out that he had the AIDS virus. However, my mother and father didn't tell us about it for about six years. We could see he was getting sicker and sicker, but they told us he had cancer. Ultimately my father sued Victory Memorial Hospital and his surgeon there for negligence for giving him AIDS-infected blood. They settled for $300,000 in 1992.

When Paul found out that he had given my father AIDS, he came to the house a short while after my father got home. My father was sitting outside on the stoop. Paul was crying and apologizing to my father. My father was very emotional. He wasn't angry at Paul at all. He was very sympathetic. He felt sorry that Paul was sick. He accepted Paul's apology and forgave him. He told Paul that it was okay, because Paul didn't know and didn't mean for it to happen. He told Paul he needed to take care of himself.

I heard part of that conversation. What stood out to me was that my father didn't make Paul feel worse than he already did. After Paul left, I asked my father what was going on. He said Paul was sick and had AIDS, but I didn't know that Paul was one of the people who had originally donated the blood. I felt bad. I told my father that it was so sad, but I still didn't know my father had AIDS, too.

My father hadn't been home from the hospital very long when he got the call that his brother, my uncle Sal, had been shot in the head. It happened at Sal's social club on Seventy-Fourth Street in the Dyker Heights sections of Brooklyn. It was about 11:50 P.M. on January 16, 1987. My mother knows more about that than me.

* * *

Right before Sal was murdered, my son was at the club with one of his best friends, Billy. Joey left because Greg had told him to be home at a certain time, but Billy was still there. He told us what happened.

"Five guys burst into the club and told everyone who was there to get down on their knees. They told Sal they wanted his pinky ring. At first, Sal refused to get on his knees, even though there was a gun pointed at his head. He relented and they shot him."

One of the gunmen was wearing a mask. The other four were African Americans, but the police said they didn't know who shot Sal. The guy who killed him said, "This is for Howard Beach." Howard Beach referred to the area where hate crimes were committed against three black men on December 19, 1986. The police said they didn't think Sal's murder was racially motivated.

Sal's watch, a gold pendant and his wallet with $313 in cash in it were found beside his body. The gunmen may have stolen the belongings of the other people in the club to make it look like a robbery, but that was all bullshit. It was a hit on Sal, and they never found out who killed him.

When my father learned he had HIV, he was kind of on the fence about what to do with his life. He maybe wanted to stop what he was doing, slow down, enjoy his family. He wanted to spend time at the Singer Island condo with my mother. He wanted to lay back and enjoy me and his grandson and my brother and his daughter. He just wanted to enjoy his life a little bit. He was sort of semiretired from the life. That's what he used to say, "I'm retired." But he always said he wouldn't hide from anyone or anything.

During that time Carmine "the Snake" Persico was the boss of the Colombo family. But in 1986 he and his son, Allie Boy, went on trial on federal racketeering charges. They were both convicted in November 1986: Carmine was sentenced to thirty-nine years in prison and Allie Boy got twelve.

Even though he was in prison, Carmine wanted to maintain control of the family until Allie Boy got out, at which point Carmine would make him boss.

In 1988, while he was still in prison, Carmine put Vittorio "Little Vic" Orena in charge of the family as acting boss. Everything seemed okay for a while, but in June 1991, Vic decided he liked being boss. That's when he announced that he was going to become the official boss of the family, even though Carmine still wanted Allie Boy to be boss when he got out of prison.

Some of the members stayed loyal to Carmine, while others were with Vic. My father hated Vic Orena, so he and his crew were backing Carmine.

Then on June 20, 1991, Carmine Sessa, the consigliere of the family, Bobby Zam and two other members of the Persico faction went to Vic's house to kill him. But the plan failed because Vic had come home early, saw the four guys near his house and took off.

Then next day Carmine Sessa walked into our house with tears in his eyes. He was crying to my father that he had had a beef with Vic Orena and Vic tried to kill him, but he got away.

My father tried to calm him down. He told Carmine that they'd straighten everything out. They sat down and Carmine started explaining to my father what had happened. My father felt a very big obligation to Carmine. He felt indebted to him. He felt strongly that he had to protect Carmine and had to help him.

As a consigliere Carmine was above my father in terms of rank. But even though he was above my father, he really wasn't above my father. My father didn't care if someone was the boss of the entire family. He wouldn't listen to him, anyway. My father was king. My father was on top of everybody. He never wanted to have that actual position of consigliere or even boss. He wanted to stay right where he was. He was happy being where he was. He knew regardless of a title or a specific position, he was going to do what he wanted, anyway. That's what he always said.

When my father first found out he had HIV, he was afraid of people coming near him. He was afraid of other people touching him. He was afraid of anybody in the family getting too close, going into his bathroom. He didn't know much about it, but he didn't want anyone to "catch" it. He was really concerned about that.

But when my father came back from the hospital after he had his stomach removed, Carmine took care of my father. He knew my father had the AIDS virus, but Carmine didn't care. He took care of him. My father had open wounds in his stomach that needed to close, and Carmine would dress the wounds. Carmine did all that for him.

My father was amazed. He couldn't believe that Carmine would actually come near him. My father felt like he had the plague. He couldn't believe that his friend was actually touching his wounds, knowing he could contract the virus. Of course, Carmine wore gloves to protect himself, but other people pretty much didn't want anything to do with my father.

My father had a really close friend, who had grown up with my mother. He and my mother had been friends their whole lives. When he and his wife found out that my father had HIV, they never spoke to my parents again.

The only other person besides Carmine who stood by my father after he got sick—and before he got sick—was my uncle Morris "Moe" Terzi, the husband of my mother's older sister, Maryann. Morris was like an older brother to my mother—he was three and a half years older than she was. From the time she was about twelve years old, he was always there for her.

My uncle Morris, who was Jewish, was my father's best friend, even though he wasn't in the life. Throughout the years he owned a number of retail clothing stores. Uncle Morris and Aunt Maryann came to the house for dinner almost every night. Because Morris was separated from the life, my father didn't have to talk business with him. He didn't have to worry about ever having a conflict with him. Their relationship was strictly a fun friendship, and one that my father really depended on.

Morris was a comedian. He had a joke for everything. When my father was feeling at his worst, Morris came to the house, made jokes and always made my father laugh. He truly was my father's best friend in life.

They met when my father first started dating my mother. But as they got older and my father got sick, that was when Morris showed his real feelings for my father. He stood by him. He helped take my father's mind off his illness.

Morris took everybody's minds off their problems. You could be sitting there crying, and Morris would walk through the door and you would just start cracking up. He would always say something or do something that was hysterical.

He was always so much fun. My brother and I loved it when he came to the house. Although he was there almost every day, we still couldn't wait to see him. Even when Morris had problems, he smiled. He was a great guy and my father really cared about him.

When my father was sick, Morris would eat, even when he didn't want to eat, just to make my father eat. Morris had to sit there and eat with him because my father didn't like to eat alone. He always wanted to have someone with him. My uncle Morris would come to the house with food, but my father would say he wasn't hungry. Uncle Morris would say, "Come on, just have a little." He would sit there and eat with my father to help him build up his immunity and gain weight. Morris got fat, but my father wasn't gaining any weight. He really couldn't, since he didn't have an actual stomach anymore.

When my uncle got diagnosed with cancer, the whole family was devastated. It was a horrible experience for everybody. Uncle Morris was the life of the party. He was the life of the family. He brought laughter to everyone. It was a major setback for my father to lose him.

When Morris was gone, there was really nobody else. His lifeline to the normal world was gone and my father was alone again. He had us and he had my mother, but he didn't have his best friend, who had been there every day to keep him company, laugh with him and eat with him.

My father was so angry because Morris had to be buried in a simple pine box, according to Jewish tradition. He thought Morris deserved better. He wanted the best for Morris, but my father wasn't Jewish and didn't understand why it had to be that way.

So Uncle Morris was the only one outside the life to be there for my father when he was sick, and Carmine was the only person in the life who came to the house day after day to take care of my father. That's why my father was so committed to Carmine.

Even though he felt a sense of responsibility to Carmine, he was still on the fence because he had the AIDS virus and didn't know how long he was going to live. He didn't know if he really wanted to get involved in a war.

After Carmine left, my father talked to my mother in the kitchen. Then he pulled me to the side to talk.

"What do you think about this?"

"Dad, do you really want to get involved with

this? What if something happens to you? What if you go to jail?"

"Linda, what do you think, I'm stupid? I don't go to jail."

"Dad, if you're going to be in the middle of this, and people are killing, and you're killing people, you don't think you're going to go to jail. You're not above the law that much."

He didn't like that. He got annoyed.

"I just want to know what you think."

"Dad, I don't know. If you think this is something that you have to do."

He wanted our permission. He wanted to do it, but he also didn't want to disappoint us if we didn't want him to do it. We really didn't want him to do it, but we didn't want to disappoint him if he wanted to do it. That's what was going on in the house.

"Dad, if you feel that you're going to be okay, you're going to be safe. . . ."

I didn't comprehend that it was going to be an all-out war. I had never been involved in a war.

"Okay, Dad. If that's what you want, just be careful."

My mother told him to do whatever he wanted to do. She knew his feelings for Carmine. He said he had to think about it. But he didn't want people to think he was soft just because he had HIV. He didn't want people to think that he was washed up—that he was done. He had to show them who was boss. He was still boss and he could still do this.

"This is the hand that has been dealt to me. I'll play the hand. If I can outbluff the opponent, which is death, fine. If I can't, I lose the hand," he said once. "I will show my enemies and my allies the bravado I have displayed all this time. I will show them that hey, this is still me. There isn't anything on this earth that I will hide from or back up from and I certainly won't do it with this, either."

So that's what he did. He decided he was going to help Carmine.

CHAPTER 9

WIND BENEATH
MY WINGS

As I've said, I always had a hard time meeting people. Everyone was afraid of my father, so I couldn't make real friends.

The only way I was able to meet guys was if they were from different neighborhoods and they didn't know who I was. And that was what happened when I met the person I married. He was a banker from Long Island, so he didn't really know a lot about my father.

The first time I met my now–ex-husband, my car had stalled on the side of the road on Eighty-Sixth Street in Brooklyn and he pulled over to help me. For a few weeks he kept calling me, asking me out. But I didn't really respond to going out with him.

My father kept asking me questions.

"Who is this guy calling? He calls every day."

"Just somebody that I met."

"Well, why don't you go out with him? He sounds like a nice guy."

So I did, and he came to the house to pick me up. That's when he first met my father. My father liked him because he wasn't from the streets. My father wanted me to settle down because he was sick, and he knew that he wasn't going to be around much longer to take care of me. He felt that this guy would be able to take care of me and do the right thing.

In the beginning my ex-husband came across as a regular guy. But down the road I found out that he wasn't such a regular guy. He wasn't a made guy, but he was into the streets more than I knew. My father knew that about six months into our relationship, but it was already too late. I had my mind set on him, and he had his mind set on me—and that was it.

We went out for about a year and then we got married in 1990, when I was twenty-one. I had told him pretty much immediately who my father was, and he didn't seem bothered by it. He didn't seem to be scared at all. Then I got pregnant and we were staying away from anything that had to do with street life. After we got married, we were really separated from all that.

The problem was that nobody was happy that we were getting married. His mother wasn't happy, and my father wasn't happy, either.

A week before my wedding my father told me not to marry the guy.

"Don't you think it's a little too late for that?"

"Don't worry about anything. I'll take care of you and the baby. I just don't want you to marry him. He's going to make you miserable."

"Dad, everything is going to be fine. Don't worry."

The wedding was like a big blur to me. I was really sick for my wedding. I had very bad morning sickness. My father was sick, too. The morning of the wedding I was afraid that I was going to pass out, and he was afraid that he was going to pass out.

My father was telling me to calm down. He was trying to keep me calm because I was so nervous that I thought I was going to faint. I had fainted once before during the pregnancy.

We got married at The Shrine Church of St. Bernadette on Thirteenth Avenue. Right before he walked me down the aisle, he said, "Calm down. Don't worry. I got you. Everything is going to be okay."

"You're telling me to calm down, and you think you're going to faint," I told him, trying to make a joke out of it. The ceremony was beautiful, and my father and I both made it through.

The wedding reception was held at La Mer on Ocean Parkway—the same place where I had my Sweet Sixteen. The hall looked so beautiful. There were gorgeous flowers on the tables. My new husband and I were glowing. When they introduced my new husband, the DJ played the theme song from *Rocky*. He came into the hall with his hands up because he was the champ.

While we were planning the wedding, my fiancé wanted to invite Gambino family boss John Gotti because his family was friends with the Gottis. My father didn't like John Gotti, so he said he couldn't come. But my fiancé said out of respect we had to leave an open seat at the reception for John Gotti, so there was an open seat. All that Gotti gave us was

$500 in an envelope, which my father thought was pretty cheap for the boss of a crime family. We did okay, though. We walked out of there with $50,000.

Until the father-daughter dance everything seemed to be going so perfectly. There was a little bit of tension at the reception because of my husband. I wasn't really all that happy, but I wanted to be. I was nervous and tense because he made me feel nervous all the time. For one thing he didn't like the fact that I kissed my father when we were dancing. He got really angry.

At that point he had a feeling that my father was sick with AIDS. He told me he had seen the medication my father was taking and it was medication for people with AIDS. But I didn't know it at that time. I thought he was crazy. I believed what my parents had told my brother and me—that my father had cancer. I didn't have any reason to doubt them.

"How do you kiss your father like that? That's disgusting."

"What are you talking about? He's my father. He kissed me while I was dancing with him."

It wasn't anything abnormal. It was a father-and-daughter kiss. That's why my father hated him so much at the end—my father knew that he was causing me all this stress.

I had a lot of regrets about my wedding. It didn't feel right. It wasn't done right. I felt that my brother was left out of a lot of it. He was in the bridal party, but that was about it. It was all about my ex's family. My father let that happen because he was trying to keep the peace, even though a week earlier he had told me not to marry him.

The song I picked for our father-daughter dance was "Wind Beneath My Wings" because of the words. My father was my hero. He was everything to me, so that was just the perfect song. But the funny part was that I couldn't figure out a song for my soon-to-be husband and me. I made the DJ pick it. He chose "All of My Life" by Aaron Neville and Linda Ronstadt.

It wasn't long before my relationship with my husband took a very big twist. Soon after we got married, things started getting strange.

We moved to Staten Island, and we were fighting like crazy over there. We were fighting all the time. My father was calling me every day to go to the house because he missed me. My husband was upset by that. He didn't want me to go. I'd bring him food that my father had cooked, but he didn't want the food from my father. He wanted me to cook. It was like he was trying to control me.

He was distancing me from my family. He was trying to keep me from them—that's why we fought. He wanted to move me to Long Island, but I wasn't ready to move there. I wanted to stay close to my father, because I didn't know how long he was going to be around.

When I was at my parents', I'd call my husband and tell him to meet me there for dinner after work. But he didn't want any part of it. He said he just wanted to go home. There was just not a good feeling. There was a lot of tension—it wasn't like a happily married couple having a baby.

That's not to say we didn't want my son. We did, very much. He was pretty much planned. We both knew what we were doing, but we were too young. We both knew that I was going to get pregnant. We were trying to get pregnant, although I'm not sure we knew why.

I guess we both wanted to get out of our situations at home. We really were not happy with our home lives. I wanted to get married—and in the beginning my father was kind of pushing me to get married. He was afraid that he wasn't going to be around long and he wanted me to find someone who would take care of me.

At the time I knew that he wasn't healthy, but I didn't know what he had. And I also knew that I didn't want to move far away from him, since I didn't know how long he was going to be around.

When I got pregnant with my son, I immediately told my parents. My mother was so excited and my father was, too. But he got all emotional, saying his baby was having a baby. When my son was born, my father came to the hospital to see the baby and me. He didn't even make it to the inside of the room.

When he saw me lying in the bed, he broke down and cried. He was so overwhelmed and filled with emotion. I felt how much he loved me at that moment, and I loved him for that. I understood that although he was so overjoyed he had a grandson from me, it hurt him to see me lying in the bed. After all, I was still his baby and now I had a baby. He couldn't stand to see me all grown-up. It bothered me to see him going through something.

My son had to stay in the hospital for a small medical issue for five days after he was born and I was a wreck. Everybody was so upset. He was so loved, especially by my father and my mother. His father and I were there with him all the time. We didn't want to leave the hospital.

On my first Valentine's Day with my husband, I decorated the whole house for him. He wasn't happy about it at all and he was very mean to me. He didn't care that I did that. He wasn't a grateful person. I used to get very upset about everything he did, but I was trying to keep it together so he wouldn't get killed. I knew if I told my father everything my husband was doing to me, he definitely would have killed him.

I did tell my father about the shirts. My husband wanted me to wash and iron his white shirts myself. My father couldn't believe it.

"It costs a dollar to get a shirt done," he said.

"Yeah, but he wants me to do them."

"Fuck that, bring them to the dry cleaner's."

"No, he's going to get mad if I do that. He doesn't like the chemicals."

"Just do me a favor. Bring me your own hangers and I'll take them to the dry cleaner's and tell them no chemicals. He'll never know the difference."

So that's what I used to do.

But it was obvious to my father that there were other problems. I was really unhappy and we weren't getting along. There were times when we would fight and my husband would somehow take both cars and leave me trapped in the house. I'd have to call my parents to come and get me.

It wasn't long before my husband and my father became almost like rivals—they didn't like each other at all. My father didn't want me with him anymore, and my husband didn't want me around my father. So I was put in the middle.

It was even more horrible because my father was sick. He would call me in the morning to go over to the house so he could make me breakfast. My husband didn't want me to go.

"You can't go. You have things to do around here. I don't want you there."

Of course, I would go, anyway, because he was my father, and my husband wasn't going to stop me from going. But it caused a lot of problems in our marriage. It pretty much broke up the marriage. My father hated him.

My father was not really as possessive as you might think he would've been. He knew that I was married and had a child. And he knew that I had to kind of figure things out—he was trying to let me do that on my own. He knew that I wasn't stupid and that I knew what was right and what was wrong for me. He saw that I wasn't happy and he saw that I was trying to do something about it on my own. I wanted my father to stay out of it.

But he couldn't do that.

One day he said, "Linda, I want to kill your husband, but I need your permission. I don't want you to live with the guilt."

"You can't do that." I was horrified. My husband was the father of my son. But, ultimately, my father was right. My husband tormented me.

I felt that the reason my father made an exception not to threaten—or kill—my husband was because we had a child together. That was probably the only reason. He felt a very strong connection to and love for my son. Knowing that my husband was his grandson's father, he was probably very torn. Still, he didn't like the way my husband was treating me anymore. I also didn't like the way I was being treated anymore, so we got divorced.

The turmoil between my father and my husband basically caused the breakup of our marriage. That and the fact that we were both very young, and we both came from homes where we were pretty spoiled. We just didn't know how to make a marriage work at that time.

Unfortunately, we were too young to know how to stick it out and work it out. I loved my husband in the beginning, but then it became such a controlling relationship. He had to control everything that I did. When I went to the store, he wanted to know why I took so long. He was just too controlling, and I was too young to be controlled. Nobody should ever be controlled, anyway.

The marriage didn't even last a year. Looking back, if I knew everything then that I know now, I probably would have tried to make it work because the pain that it caused my son growing up was pretty bad.

Ten years after I was divorced, I met someone else—someone I had known when we were kids. But we had moved away from him when I was sixteen.

We met up again when I was in my thirties and we hit it off immediately. I felt such a sense of security with him. Here was somebody who knew my whole life story. He knew my family. Someone I didn't have to explain myself to—someone who was going to be good to me.

We ended up living together and I had three children with him. And during the time that we were together, he became extremely abusive. I became a victim of domestic violence. After all of the years of having everything, and being protected, and thinking that no one could ever hurt me, I was the victim of domestic violence. I was walking around on eggshells every day, waking up afraid.

This guy wasn't a street guy at all. He had been a straight-A student in high school. Very smart, good-looking, educated, went to law school. He was the person I went to when I needed help with homework as a kid. He wasn't from the streets, but there was something just not right with him. He would constantly bring up my father and call me names. He called me a rat and said I came from a rat family.

He was so abusive and I was so afraid of him that I wouldn't even prosecute him until one of the assaults was so bad that I had no choice. The district attorney told me they weren't going to need me on the witness stand because they were going to have my body on a slab and that would have been enough for them to put him away. I was afraid I was going to die, so I decided to testify.

Finally after thirty-five arrests for assaulting me, he went to prison. It was kind of ironic that my life would take such a twist. My father had protected me when I was growing up, but then he was gone and I was the victim of abuse. If my father had been alive for that, only God knows what he would've done.

CHAPTER 10

THE SHOOTING ON THE BLOCK

It was November 18, 1991—a cold late-fall day. There was a very eerie feeling in the air. It was scary—a day I'll never forget.

It had been five months since the war erupted and things seemed kind of peaceful. Little did I know, all hell was about to break loose.

When the war was going on, there was a lot of tension in the air. There were a lot of people at my house all the time—my father's crew never left his side. They'd come to the house armed—each one had his own weapons—to pick him up. Then they'd go wherever they had to go. They'd drive around the neighborhood, go to the club. They were always on guard.

My father usually left the house at the same time every day—between eleven o'clock and noon. That was his routine. On this particular day I happened to leave at the same time as my father, which I never did. I had a shower to go to that night and I was going to buy a gift. I was walking down the steps carrying the baby, who was eight months old, and his diaper bag. And walking all around me were all these guys with loaded pistols. I couldn't see the guns, but I knew they all had them.

I know that's crazy, but at the time it all seemed perfectly normal. I wasn't thinking, *Holy shit, I'm surrounded by guys with guns.* Back then this really was kind of normal for me.

When I got to my black Mercedes, which was parked in front of the house, my father helped me put the baby into his car seat and kissed us good-bye. As soon as my son was settled, I got into my car. My father got into his car, which was parked in the driveway.

His car pulled out of the driveway and took a right heading toward Twelfth Avenue. I checked my rearview mirror and saw a van speeding up the block. When I backed out, I cut the van off. It almost slammed into me because it was so close and the driver was trying to pass me. I didn't have any idea who it was. I was thinking it was just a van driving up the block, but the guy was really flying. I yelled a few choice words and started driving again.

As I got to the corner of the block, where Eighty-Second Street met Twelfth Avenue, I saw a big white truck pull in horizontally between the stop signs on both sides of the street. My father's car got to the stop sign and my car was right behind him. The van was behind me. For some reason I glanced over to look at the baby, who was next to me in his rear-facing car seat.

At that moment I noticed this statue of Jesus in the front yard of the house on my left—his arms outstretched toward me and my son—surrounded by perfectly manicured shrubs. It was in front of this magnificent tree. Dried-up brown leaves still clinging to its nearly bare branches, remnants of summer. The statue had been there forever, but I never really paid much attention.

My father's car came to an abrupt stop, forcing me to stop my car. Since we weren't going anywhere, I figured it was a good time to put my radio back into the dash. Everybody was stealing car radios at that time, so Mercedes made radios that you could remove from the dashboard. I leaned down and reached underneath my seat, where I used to stash my radio. All of a sudden I heard popping noises that sounded just like fireworks.

I looked up and there were these guys dressed from head to toe in black. It was like a scene from a Mafia movie, but it was all too real. Their faces were covered with black ski masks and they were carrying these long black guns with silencers. They literally were dressed to kill.

They surrounded our cars and they started shooting at my father's car. As soon as the first shots rang out, I saw my father go down. I couldn't see him anymore. I was in shock. I was convinced my father was dead. Was I dead, too? Was I going to get killed right then? What was going to happen to my son and me?

I wanted to take him out of his car seat and put him on the floor, but I was too afraid to move or move him. I put my hand on him. *Oh, my God, what am I going to do?* I was only twenty-two years old.

The fear was paralyzing. Everything happened so fast, but the minutes felt like hours. It was like I was outside my body, watching everything that was going on around me. I noticed this one guy with a walkie-talkie standing on the sidewalk, to the right of our cars, watching this whole thing as if he was directing a movie. I didn't know who he was. He had salt-and-pepper hair and very thick eyebrows. He was wearing a black trench coat and a black hat. I couldn't believe he was just standing there, watching these guys shooting at my father's car.

One of my father's friends, Joe Fish, hopped out of my father's car. He was the only one who got out. Joe started shooting back. One of the guys, who was to the right of my car, started shooting back at Joe. Joe had his hair styled in a DA, and I saw the wind from the bullet whiz right through it. He just missed getting his head blown up. I read his lips. He said, "Holy shit." He must have felt it, because he immediately jumped back in the car.

The guy he was shooting at panicked. His automatic gun was spraying bullets everywhere. He even shot into my car. By now my father's entire car looked like Swiss cheese. It was a miracle no one got killed. All those guys must have been amateurs, because they didn't even hit anybody. It was like the gang that couldn't shoot straight.

The next thing I knew, the car my father was in took off. There was a slight gap between the stop sign and the truck. The guy who was driving the car, Ilario "Fat Larry" Sessa, didn't care if he took all the doors off the car. He was going to get the hell out of there. He made it through. I found out later that all the while father was screaming, "Stop the fucking car! What are you crazy? My daughter is back there." But Larry wasn't stopping the car. He was gunning it. He was scared.

So my father slapped him. "Stop the fucking car and let me out. My daughter is over there!" he screamed. But Larry still didn't want to let my father out. Finally he stopped the car, and my father got out and started walking back to us.

While all this was happening, I didn't have a clue where he was. I was convinced he was dead in his car. I was left there on the road—the baby and I— with the van, the truck, the guy on the sidewalk in the trench coat and all these guys dressed in black. My heart was in my mouth. I knew I was I going to die right then. They were going to kill me.

Then one of the guys—I'll never forget him because he had the bluest eyes—the guy whose gun was spraying bullets, came running over to my car. All the other guys started scattering and running away, except for the guy directing the hit on the sidewalk. He just nonchalantly started walking away like nothing ever happened.

The guy with the blue eyes came running over to me. I looked at him; he looked at me; time stood still. I didn't know if he was going to shoot me in the head, but he just looked at me. Maybe it was because he knew his gun had sprayed into my car and he wanted to see if I got hit. He looked into the car; then he turned and ran away.

When the gunshots stopped, there was dead silence. I had the sickest feeling. As soon as the guy ran, and all that crazy energy was gone, my son started screaming.

I was shaking. Blue eyes let me live. Did he purposely let me live? Did he want to see if I was okay? Did he think he got my son or me? Did he have an ounce of a heart to check on us? I've never stopped wondering about that.

I was left there alone. I didn't know what to do. Should I go to the store, or should I go home? I was in such a state of shock. I couldn't think straight.

When reality set in about what had just happened to us, I slammed the car into reverse and backed up to the house as fast as I could. I pulled into my spot in the driveway, shut the car off and grabbed my son out of his car seat. As I was getting the baby and my bag out of the car, the guy in the trench coat walked right by me.

I started running up to the house. I had no strength. I was dropping stuff—my keys, my bags—as I went. How I didn't drop my son, I'll never know. I felt completely drained. I had no strength left in my body to hold anything. But I held on to my son until I got to the door. I pulled on the door handle, but it was locked. I didn't know where my keys were.

I started ringing the bell and banging on the door, screaming. "Ma, Ma, open the door! Open the fucking door!" All of a sudden she opened the door and I dropped my son in her arms. I just couldn't hold him any longer. I wanted to fall on the floor.

"What happened? What's going on?"

"Mom, I think they killed Daddy. I think they killed Daddy."

"What are you talking about?"

I started freaking out. "Oh, my God! Oh, my God!" I screamed. Then I started ranting and raving. "There was a truck and there were guys. They were shooting at Daddy. I think he's dead. I think he's dead," I said, sobbing uncontrollably.

"Is he dead? Do you know?"

"I don't know. I think they killed him. They were shooting at the car."

I was going wild, totally freaking out—screaming. And the baby was still screaming. My mother was trying to calm me down.

"Calm down, we have to think," she said.

"Think about what, Mom? How are we going to find out what happened to Daddy?"

The next thing I knew, my father walked through the door. He was pale as a ghost. He saw me and the baby and he just started to cry. He grabbed my son and hugged him. Then he looked at me.

"You saved my life. You realize that, right?"

If I hadn't pulled out and cut off the van, my father and everybody in his car would have been dead. The four guys in the car—they would have been done.

"Dad . . . oh, my God. Oh, my God. I can't believe they didn't get you. What happened?"

"I ducked down," he said. "Don't worry. Everything's okay."

"What do you mean? Everything's not okay."

"Don't worry," he said, trying to calm me down.

"What do you mean, 'don't worry'?"

"Don't worry, I'm going to take care of this."

Then he looked at my mother. "They're all fucking dead. They're going to fucking die, starting tonight."

"Greg, calm down," my mother said.

"*Calm down?* They're fucking dead."

When my father walked through the door and saw that my son and I were safe, I saw the love in his eyes and the fear that his child and grandchild could have been hurt or killed. That was the look of my father.

But as soon as he knew we were okay, he had the look of the devil in his eyes—and he never, ever lost it until the day he died.

CHAPTER 11

OPERATION WILD BILL

After the shooting on the block, my father wanted to know exactly who was involved, so he called Lin DeVecchio. He wanted to know what Lin had heard. My father didn't call him as his FBI handler; he called him as his friend.

My father gave him the license plate number of one of the trucks used in the shooting. Lin checked around. He told my father that the truck belonged to William "Wild Bill" Cutolo. So my father knew that Wild Bill and Vic Orena had called the hit—and now he knew who his targets were.

One day not long after that, we were all sitting at the table—me, my mother, my father, Larry Mazza, Jimmy Delmasto, and their wives or girlfriends. The television was turned to the news and there was a story about Operation Desert Storm, which my father was watching.

When it was over, he turned to me.

"Linda, when you go out tomorrow, I want you to do me a favor and go to the store for me."

"For what?"

"I want you to get me—you know those baseball hats? The ones that you can put letters on?"

"Yeah."

"Get me the iron-on letters that say 'Operation Wild Bill.'"

"Dad, you're joking, right? You can't wear that."

"No, really, I want to wear it."

"Dad, you can't wear that."

"I'm wearing it. Could you get it for me?"

"Dad, how am I going to walk into a store and ask for that?"

"Why? What's the big deal? Just get me the hat with the letters. They're not going to know what it's for."

"I don't know, Dad. All right, yeah, I'll get it for you."

I had to do what he said; we really couldn't say no to him at that point. If we said no, we'd get into a lot of trouble. It was never like that before.

"Okay, Dad, I'll get you the hat, no problem. I have to look for it. I have to find a place that has them. I don't even know where to get it."

Larry and Jimmy were laughing about this hat that I had to get, but the fact was my father wanted Wild Bill and his son dead as much as he wanted Vic Orena and his sons dead.

A few nights after my father told me to get the hat, my cousin's husband came over to house and he was wearing a beautiful new black coat. My father took one look at it and said, "John, let me see that coat."

"What do you mean? I just got the coat. I'll tell you where I got it."

"No, I want to try it on. I want to see if it fits me."

John had no idea why my father wanted to see the coat, but he handed it over. My father tried it on. Then he took a wad of cash out of his pocket and handed it to John.

"Here's some money. Go buy yourself a new coat."

I was sitting on the couch, watching *Wheel of Fortune.* My father turned to me and said, "Linda, go get me the scissors."

"Greg, what are you doing with my coat? I just got the coat," John said. "It's freezing out and I need a coat."

"No, this is my coat now. I need the coat."

After I gave him the scissors, he cut the right pocket out of the coat. Then he got his shotgun and put it in the pocket.

"Perfect. Look at this, Linda. The gun fits perfect. They'll never even know. John, can you get me a Jewish hat and a beard like the Jews wear?"

"Seriously?" John asked, really confused.

My father was looking at himself with the coat, admiring his handiwork.

"Look, all I have to do is poke the gun out. *Boom!* It's perfect, this coat. Thanks, pal," my father said to John, giving him a pat on the back. "Thanks for the coat."

A few days after that, my father and my mother were talking about Wild Bill. They were in the kitchen; I was in the living room.

"He's staying at his girlfriend's house, so we're

going to go there and we're going to get him at his girlfriend's house," my father said.

"How did Lin find out that he's at his girlfriend's house?" my mother asked, referring to Lin DeVecchio.

"Come on, Lin." He called her "Lin" sometimes, too. "You're joking around, right?"

"No. How did he know where he's hiding?"

"Well, he found out, and that's where he is, so we're going to get him there."

My father's plan was that he and his crew would dress up like Hasidic Jews and murder Wild Bill on Thanksgiving in front of his girlfriend's grandmother's house in a Hasidic neighborhood in Brooklyn. But he had to call off the hit because of an article that ran in the *New York Post* on Thanksgiving morning that speculated that my father was a rat. He had to spend some time convincing the other members of the Colombo family that he was no such thing.

During that part of the war I kept going back and forth to my aunt's house on Eightieth Street because I was so scared. One day when I was there, my father called me up and said, "I miss you. Come home."

"Dad, I'm scared."

"No, I miss you. Everything's okay. Just come home."

So, of course, I went home because he missed me and he missed my son. Screw my safety—I wasn't thinking about that. I was thinking that my father missed me and I had to go home. I couldn't really stay away from him because he had a way of calling me and making me feel guilty. But deep down I missed him, too.

So I went. One night after I had been home for a

few days, I had this dream. I woke up and I was freaking out. The dream started out exactly the way I said good night to my father every night.

When I went up to bed, I always kissed my father good night; or if he went to bed before me, I went over to him and kissed him good night as he walked up the steps. The dream started off after I kissed him good night and went to bed. The next thing I knew—in my dream—there were these guys coming through the window dressed in the same black outfits as the guys who tried to kill my father.

I hid under my blankets, thinking in my dream that they weren't going to see me. Then they went into my mother's room and killed my mother and father. I heard the gunshots and the screaming. Then they went into my brother Joey's room and killed him. Then they came back into my room, and that's when I woke up, screaming.

My father came rushing into my room to comfort me.

"I can't take this anymore," I said. "I can't live like this."

I was scared. I was traumatized. I thought my father was going to die.

"They're going to kill you," I said to him.

"No one is going to kill your father," he said.

"Dad, you don't know that. They almost killed you."

"Linda, believe me, they're not killing me. I'm going to get every one of those fucking bastards. Do you think I'm going to let them kill me? You don't know your father?"

He always said that: "You don't know your father?"

"Dad, they're going to get you eventually. It's going to happen. And I don't want to see that happen. I don't want you to leave me. Please don't leave me."

"Linda, I'm not going nowhere. Relax. Listen, I have to end this. I'm not going to walk away. I have to end this."

"Dad, it's not going to end the way you think."

"This is what I have to do. This is what I have to do."

He just didn't care anymore about how I felt. He didn't care that his family was being destroyed. He was so juiced up. He was a killing machine and his goal was to kill all those involved.

Before, if he had to kill somebody, he'd do it and then come home, eat dinner with his family and go to bed. Then he'd wake up in the morning and it would be a normal day. But during the war it was like killing was his only purpose.

"I have to do this. I have to defend this family," he said.

But he didn't mean just our family. He meant the Persico family. Screw the Persico family! What did they ever do for us but put us in that position? But he had to defend them, and that was what he was living by.

Today I realize that if he didn't have AIDS, he would have been thinking more logically. But because he knew he was going to die of AIDS, he'd always say, "I don't want to die of this disease." His thinking was that if he had to die by the bullet or by the disease, he'd rather take the bullet.

CHAPTER 12

AIDS—GREG SCARPA'S MOST POWERFUL WEAPON

As for us—after the shooting, that was the end of anything normal in our family. That was the end of it all. My life, as I knew it, was gone. Even though my father always talked to us about his life, he still tried to keep the family as normal as it could be. What I thought was normal was gone.

Before the shooting I had a mother and a father and a brother. And we were a family. When I woke up in the morning, I could pick up the phone and know that they would be there. But everything was gone—there was nothing left.

Greg Junior was already in jail, but the same guys put out a hit on him in jail for the same day that they tried to kill my father. It was supposed to be my father and Gregory. Gregory got stabbed in the neck, but he lived.

After the hit my father sent Joey away to a farm in upstate New Jersey. My father didn't want him involved in the war. He knew if his enemies saw Joey in the streets, they were going to kill him.

At that point I didn't have the same feeling that I had when I was younger, that my father was invincible and no one could ever touch him. Now I knew that my father wasn't invincible, and neither were we. We were open game in that life. Nobody was protected, and nobody was safe.

Even though the guys were in the same crime family, they didn't care. They were killing each other. They didn't care about killing a guy in front of his wife or children anymore. There was no loyalty in the family. They didn't care that I was there. They didn't care that my son was in the car. They knew and they didn't care.

As far as my father was concerned, they crossed the line in that world when they attempted to kill him in front of his grandson and me. So everybody was fair game to him; he didn't care if there was an innocent person standing next to the person that he wanted.

For him, it was revenge. But also on top of his revenge, he was sick with AIDS. He wasn't thinking clearly because he was on such heavy medications, which distorted his perception. Even though he was so distraught over the shooting, he might have handled it differently, if he hadn't been so sick.

The way he handled it, he was just out of control. He wanted to get anybody he could who was on the other side. He just didn't care. He didn't care if he didn't come home at night, and that was the scariest part for my brother and me—not knowing if he was going to come home. We knew he was going out. We knew what he was going to do. We didn't know if he was going to return home.

My father wasn't going quietly, until he got everybody who was involved. And he had to deal with the nightmares that I was having. I was screaming and crying all the time. I was too afraid to walk around. I was afraid to do anything. I was afraid to leave the house.

Once those people tried to kill him in front of us, he became an absolute irate maniac. There was no stopping my father. You couldn't talk to him the same anymore. Not me, not my mother—no one could tell him what to do at that point. You couldn't control him. He was a different person. He became a killing machine and he didn't care about anything.

He did care about us, but he wasn't the father I knew anymore. He was on a mission to get revenge and that was the bottom line. He wanted them—Vic Orena's crew and Wild Bill's crew. He called up Larry Mazza, because Larry hadn't been with him the day of the shooting, and Jimmy Delmasto. They were the first ones who came to the house and then the rest of the crew came over.

That afternoon I called my ex-husband. I told him I needed his help. I said his son and I needed a place to stay. Basically, he said we were on our own.

"What do you mean I'm on my own?" I screamed into the telephone. "This just happened to me and your son, and you're telling me you don't have a place for us to stay?"

He said we couldn't stay with him.

Now all of my father's crew were in the living room. They were all armed. There were guns that I never even knew existed. I had no idea a civilian could even have access to those kinds of weapons.

I was scared. I tried talking to my father, but he wasn't listening.

"Dad, I can't stay here."

"You're not going anywhere."

"Dad, I'm not staying here. I'm scared. You got all these guys here."

"Where are you going to go?"

"I don't know, but I can't stay here, Dad. I'm scared."

So he told me to call my aunt, the one who lived on Eightieth Street, and ask if I could stay with her for a while. She agreed; so the next day I took my son and we left. We were back a few days later.

That night in our house my father gave his crew their orders.

"This is what you're doing—you're all going out and you're going to be in different cars. Whenever you see somebody, you kill them. I don't care if they're with their mother or their father, their sister, their daughter. I don't care. If you see one of these people, you fucking kill them," he said.

"What do you mean if we see them with somebody?" one of the guys asked.

"They wanted to kill me in front of my daughter and my grandchild. I don't care who they're fucking with. And if I find out that you seen somebody who was with someone—their mother—and you didn't get them, you're going to have to fucking answer to me. You're going to answer to me, so make sure you do what I'm telling you to do."

My father felt that the guy in the trench coat with the walkie-talkie saw me and knew who I was. He could have called off the hit because I was there, but he didn't. The plan was in place and ready, and they decided to do it whether I was there or not. And now my father didn't care about their families, either.

So they went out that night and from then on it was day after day, night after night. They were on a mission to kill people. During the war, my father spoke about the people he killed openly in front of my family as if he expected us to know who this person was, or who that guy was and we had to deal with it.

He once said, "When you choose this life, you choose to live or die—some people live, some people die, but this is the life we chose." The war was complete mayhem—the killing was all over the news. People were getting sloppy and so hungry for revenge. The guys from both factions were waiting just to kill.

Although my father was sick with AIDS and his once-muscular body had shriveled from 225 pounds to just 150, he and his crew cruised along Avenue U in Brooklyn, looking for members of the Orena faction in social clubs and bars. He was particularly looking for Wild Bill, since he had orchestrated the hit on him.

Over the next few weeks the bullets flew and the bodies piled up.

On November 24, Persico soldier Hank Smurra was murdered. On November 29, Fat Larry was ambushed in a drive-by shooting. Fat Larry wasn't hit, but the driver of the car he was riding in hit several pedestrians, including a four-year-old girl, as it made its getaway.

Every day during the war was a day of hunting—searching and hunting—for my father. Day in and day out, and during the night, until he was satisfied—and he wasn't going to be satisfied until he killed every one of them.

On Tuesday morning, December 3, 1991, my father was out hunting with Larry and Jimmy when he saw Orena loyalist Joey Tolino standing in front of a social club in the Gravesend section of Brooklyn. Tolino was standing with this old guy, Gaetano "Tommy Scar" Amato. He was seventy-eight and was a member of the Genovese family, not the Colombo family.

As Jimmy was driving the van in front of the club, my father started shooting. The bullets were flying. He only wounded Joey, who was the target, but he accidentally killed Tommy.

I remember when my father came home that day. He was pissed off and aggravated. I asked him what was wrong, and he told me that he shot the wrong guy.

"What do you mean?"

"Well, there was a guy that I wanted to get. He was with the Orenas. And I fired, and I shot the wrong guy."

He sat down and turned on the TV. He was pretty distraught that he had killed the wrong person. I sat down next to him and we talked about it. He said Tommy was a nice guy. I was sorry that it happened and I felt bad for my father that he felt so bad. My father said Tommy was a family man, and he didn't mean to hurt him and it was done accidentally. I tried to comfort him.

"But, Dad, he was in the wrong place at the wrong time."

How twisted is that? My thought process was distorted. Why would I say such a thing? My father just looked at me, confused. He didn't know how I could say something like that, and neither did I. It just came out. I had never seen my father show remorse before and I just wanted to help him.

When I saw Tommy's obituary in the paper, I was really upset. He was described as a father and a grandfather who was loved and who would be missed.

As I was reading it, I thought I could be reading about my father. He was going out killing people, and someone could just as easily kill him. Just thinking about it was driving me crazy. I didn't want anything to happen to my father. I didn't want him to be involved in this war.

I actually approached him about it.

"Dad, you're not invincible. What if something happens to you? What if they get you?"

He got really pissed at me.

"No one is getting me. What do you think, your father is stupid?"

He wasn't in his right frame of mind because of the AIDS dementia. He wasn't acting like a sympathetic father anymore—he was becoming an offensive killer.

"What do you think, I'm stupid? I'm not a stupid guy. Nobody is fucking getting me. They tried once—shame on them. They ain't gonna get another shot at me."

He was getting agitated with me. And that was hard for me to come to grips with, because I was getting angry toward him for making us go through this. It was very traumatic for my brother and me at that time. The months were dragging on, and it was just the same thing day after day—him going out and trying to kill people.

Two days later, on December 5, Persico soldier Rosario Nastasi was shot dead while he was playing cards in a social club in Bay Ridge and his girlfriend was wounded.

The next day my father killed Vincent Fusaro, an Orena loyalist, while he was hanging Christmas lights outside his family's home. The story was that Fusaro was standing on a ladder, with his back facing the street. So my father rolled down his car window and stuck his rifle out, getting off three shots that found their target.

On December 8, James Malpeso, a member of the Orena faction, was shot in the chest. Several days later, in retaliation for that hit, the Orena crew murdered eighteen-year-old Matteo Speranza, who was working behind the counter at the Wanna Bagel store on Third Avenue in Bay Ridge. That was another mistake. They were gunning for another employee.

After that happened, my father came home and talked about this young kid who got killed in a bagel store. He said he was an innocent kid just working in a store that was owned by a Persico—the Persico family had a piece of this bagel store. My father

My father, Greg Scarpa Sr., was always my hero.
Here he is with me at my wedding.
(Photo courtesy of Linda C. Schiro)

Even at nineteen, my father wanted to live the good life.
(Photo by Sal Scarpa)

By his mid-twenties, my father was already involved with the mob.
(Photo by Sal Scarpa)

My gorgeous mother out to dinner with my father when she was twenty years old.
(Photo by Greg Scarpa)

That's me with my father and my grandfather, Sam Diana.
(Photo courtesy of Linda C. Schiro)

Feeling safe and loved in my father's arms.
(Photo courtesy of Linda C. Schiro)

Celebrating my first Holy Communion.
(Photo courtesy of Linda C. Schiro)

Six years old and I had a rabbit coat.
I didn't like it because the rabbits had to die.
(Photo courtesy of Linda C. Schiro)

My brother, Joey, and me holding hands.
I was very protective of him when we were kids.
But I couldn't protect him forever.
(Photo courtesy of Linda C. Schiro)

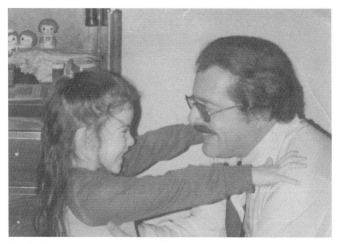

I was always
Daddy's little girl.
*(Photo courtesy of
Linda C. Schiro)*

Hanging out
with my father.
I always wanted
to be with him.
*(Photo courtesy of
Linda C. Schiro)*

Dancing with my father to "Daddy's Little Girl" at my Sweet 16 party.
(Photo courtesy of Linda C. Schiro)

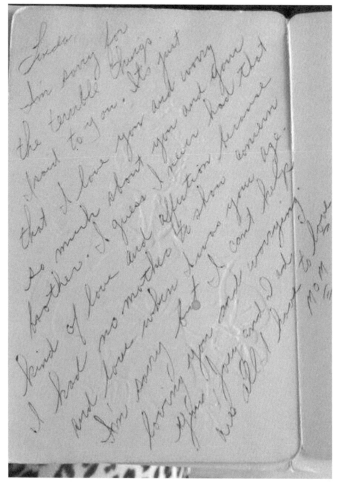

A letter my mother wrote to me shortly after my father
and his crew beat up my friend Greg Vacca.
(Photo courtesy of Linda C. Schiro)

My mother all dolled up and looking glamorous at our house.
(Photo by Greg Scarpa)

Uncle Sal Scarpa joking around with my father,
who does not look amused.
(Photo courtesy of Linda C. Schiro)

My father and his grandson, Gregory Scarpa III.
(Photo courtesy of Linda C. Schiro)

Our parents made Christmas a magical time for my brother and me.
(Photo courtesy of Linda Scarpa)

Sharing a special moment. Joey idolized our father.
(Photo courtesy of Linda C. Schiro)

Celebrating my birthday. Having my father with me
was the best present. *(Photo courtesy of Linda C. Schiro)*

I hated seeing my father so sick, but I had to put on a brave face for him. *(Photo courtesy of Linda C. Schiro)*

You once said that I was your hero I have since learned that you are my hero

Love you
DAD
(K.M.)

A letter my father wrote to me when he was suffering from AIDS-related dementia. He signed it with the initials K.M., which stands for Killing Machine. He never would have written that if he hadn't been sick.

said that because the Orena faction wasn't getting anybody, they were becoming frustrated. So they went to this bagel store and decided, "You know what? We're just gonna kill the kid who works in the store."

My father was pissed. He was ranting and raving that the Orena crew was out of control and needed to be put in their place. He was really going nuts about this poor kid, who was completely and totally innocent, getting killed.

During this part of the war my father was getting information about the Orena faction from Lin DeVecchio, despite what Lin would like to have people believe.

On January 7, 1992, my father murdered Nicholas "Nicky Black" Grancio, one of the capos in the Orena faction. That was the worst one for me to hear about.

My mother was there when Larry and Jimmy came to the house to tell my father that they had just seen Nicky Black on Avenue U: "Larry came to the house with Jimmy and told Greg he had just seen Nicky on Avenue U, but there was police surveillance around. Then Greg got on the phone and got in touch with Lin, and then the surveillance wasn't there anymore. So when Greg, Larry and Jimmy went back to Avenue U, there was nobody around, and that's why they had the opportunity to kill Nicky Black.

"And he got Nicky Black, shot him in the face, while Nicky was sitting in his SUV with his nephew. When he came back with Larry, Greg got on the phone with Lin and told him, 'This was the big one.'"

Nicky Black was my father's prize kill. He was like his twelve-point buck. Because to him, as far as status in the family, Nicky Black was the biggest one.

So when he walked through the door, my father came in like a hunter who had bagged a deer. He was psyched.

"You had to see it. You had to fucking see it. You had to see. I shot his nose right off his face. There was blood all over the windows. I literally shot his nose off his fucking face, that rat bastard."

My father was freaking out that he had killed Nicky, and the blood, and the nose, and this and that, and ranting and raving about it.

"Fuck them, I'm gonna show them who's the boss! I'm gonna fucking win this thing for Allie."

But then he changed. It was like he didn't really care about anybody. It was about taking care of himself.

"Fuck Allie, too. You know what? This ain't even about Allie anymore. This is about me. This is about what they did to me. This is about what they did to my family. Fuck everybody."

I sat there looking at him—this crazed man—and I was literally scared of my own father.

My father was involved in another shooting. The guy's name was Joel "Joe Waverly" Cacace. Waverly was part of the Orena faction, so my father hated him. But he hated him even before the war and he wanted him dead, anyway. War or no war, it didn't matter. Killing Waverly would have been a trophy for him.

Sometime in January 1992, my father was out

hunting in Brooklyn with Larry Mazza and Jimmy Delmasto. They pulled up alongside Joe Waverly's car. They opened the window so my father could shoot him, but the gun got stuck. It didn't fire. Waverly shot back, but he missed them. Nobody in the car got hit that day. But if they hadn't gotten out of there fast, they could have been killed.

After that, they came home and were laughing about it. They thought it was pretty funny. They were saying things like: "I can't believe what happened to the gun. This is nuts. That was crazy. Holy shit!"

I was just sitting there in the living room, listening to them. I couldn't believe what I was hearing. The whole thing was entertaining to them. Just a little before that happened, Larry and Jimmy had both just had babies. So it was shocking to me to witness them become killers, because they had just become fathers. I really thought their kids and their families would have taken priority over them becoming full-fledged hit men.

Most men would have felt the need to go to work to provide for and protect their new babies and families and learn how to be fathers. But these guys found the need to go to war to protect their Mob family, the Persico faction, and learn how to be Mob killers.

I grew up around these guys. They were always fun and loving guys, listening to Elvis, listening to music, playing card games in the house, making jokes and laughing all the time. I was so confused how some of these guys could flip a switch and become the type of people to take another life and show no remorse.

But then again I watched this, growing up around my father—he never showed remorse, either. It was second nature to him, and it came so natural. So being around that, being in that life, I felt these guys learned how to kill and show no feelings.

They were taking this war seriously. They had my father's back and were going out and killing people with my father—and enjoying it.

So they missed Joe Waverly, and, of course, that didn't sit well with my father. That meant they had to go back and get him another time, which they did.

So on February 26, 1992, my father took the family car, which was a black Mercedes-Benz, and went looking for Joe Waverly—but I didn't know he did that at the time. To me, that's pretty sick—to take a car that your kids drive and go and shoot somebody on Avenue U.

But that's what he did. He saw Joe Waverly in front of the Party Room Social Club on Avenue U and shot him. He didn't care that he had the family car. That's what he wanted to do. Period. The end. Joe Waverly shot back, but he missed my father. My father shot him in the stomach, but he didn't kill him.

When my father came home, he told us what happened, never mentioning he was driving the family car.

"I shot him, but I fucking didn't kill the guy. But that's all right. He'll be damaged for the rest of his life."

I'm not sure how he knew that—maybe because of where he shot him.

As all of this was happening, my father gave me certain instructions. All of a sudden I had rules. He told me I wasn't allowed to drive on certain avenues, such as Avenue U, and I wasn't allowed to drive at night.

After he shot Joe Waverly, my father and my mother told me not to take the family car out, but they didn't tell me why. So, of course, I took the car out. I had no idea that he had taken the car to go shoot somebody—he didn't tell me that part!

I took the car and drove to Lester's clothing store on Avenue U. I was driving back to the house on Eighty-Second Street. I think I was somewhere around Eighty-Fourth Street and Twentieth Avenue when I noticed this car behind me. It was another Mercedes. The lights were on because it was around five in the afternoon and it was dark. And then the lights went off, and I was scared.

When I got to the stop sign, this guy pulled the car up next to me. He opened his window and motioned for me to roll down my window. Stupidly, I rolled down my window.

"Whose car is that?"

"Why?"

"I'm just wondering whose car that is."

I decided to answer him because I knew this was going to be a problem.

"This is my father's car."

"Oh, really? Why are you driving your father's car?"

"Well, because it's my father's car, and I think I can drive it."

I was acting all tough, but meanwhile I was shitting myself.

There were two guys in the car—one was a good-looking guy, dark with very dark hair. The other one was light-skinned, with light hair and light eyes. He kept telling the dark-haired guy, "Leave her alone. Leave her alone."

"What's the matter? You look scared," the dark-haired guy said.

"Yeah, well, you pull up next to me, you shut your lights and you're asking me questions. Yeah, you scared me a little."

"Yeah, well, you have reason to be scared."

"I do? Why?"

The light-haired guy told him again to leave me alone.

But then the dark-haired guy took out a pocket-knife from somewhere and held it in his hand. He put his hand on the steering wheel so I could see the knife.

Then the blond guy said, "Just leave her alone. Come on, let's go."

"All right, you know what? I'll leave you alone. Take care." And then he drove away.

I drove home as fast as I could. The first thing I did was tell my parents what had happened. My father—and my mother—started screaming at me.

"I told you not to take that car out!"

"Why? What's the big fucking deal with the car?"

Then they told me.

"Oh, my God. This could've just ended up tragic for me! I'm driving around in a car you just shot someone in? Holy shit!"

"What kind of car was it? And what did he look like?"

I described the guy to my father, but he said he wasn't sure who it was.

Everything was out of control—really out of control. But that's how it was in the neighborhood, even driving in my own car. It was very eerie. All the time, I was watching out behind me. Watching over my shoulder. Always looking around. Always afraid. Not knowing if somebody was going to take something out on my brother or me. So that's how we lived for those months when the war was happening.

A few weeks later I had to take my son to the doctor's office because he had a cold. I was sitting by the window in the office, and who did I see? The guy with the dark hair who had pulled up next to my car. But he was with a whole bunch of guys, and they went into the same building where the doctor's office was.

I called up my father.

"Dad, the guy who pulled up next to me is coming into this building with a whole bunch of guys, like for a meeting."

"Well, where's the doctor's office?"

After I told him, he said, "Well, I don't know who it is, Linda."

"But, Dad, this is the guy who pulled up next to me."

I found out later, on my own, that he was Nicky Black's son. One day I was driving in Brooklyn and I saw the car parked in front of the house of a girl I knew. I didn't really like her and we didn't talk very much, but I knew who she was.

One day I saw her on the street and I started talking to her.

"Whose car is that at your house? It's a really nice car," I said.

"Oh, that's . . . I forget his name. I don't know if it's Nicky."

Then she said that he was Nicky Black's son.

"Isn't he so hot? He lives in my house."

"Oh, yeah. He's really good-looking," I agreed.

I didn't ask what she was talking about, and I really didn't care. I was just trying to find out who he was.

When I got home, I told my father.

"Dad, that's Nicky Black's son, who did that."

"How do you know?"

Then I told him the story.

"Well, at least we know who it is."

I was thinking that he was probably going to kill him because of what he did to me and because he was on the other side. I was also afraid he was going to kill another guy who was with the Orena faction— a guy I liked.

"Well, Dad, listen. There's this guy that I'm friends with, and he's not on your side. I don't want you to hurt him."

"Who is it?"

"His name is Tommy Cappa, and I don't want you doing anything to him."

"I know Tommy Cappa, but why don't you want me doing anything to him?"

"Because I like him, and I don't want you doing anything to him. He's my friend, and I don't want you to kill him."

"Linda, if I see him, I'm killing him."

"Dad, I don't want you to kill him. There's other people for you to kill. Can you not get him? Please don't do anything to him."

This was the conversation I was having with my father. Tommy was young. He was about my age, maybe a couple years older, so maybe twenty-three or twenty-four. I liked him, and I didn't want anything to happen to him. My father said he didn't care who it was. He was killing anyone who was with the Orenas. Still, I begged my father not to hurt this kid.

During one of the days he was out hunting with Larry and Jimmy, he saw Tommy Cappa. He pulled up alongside the guy's car at a red light. Tommy looked up and saw death right in front of him. My father let him go, though.

When he came home that day, my father told me what had happened.

"Guess who I saw today?"

"Who?"

"I seen Tommy."

"Dad, tell me you didn't."

"No, I didn't touch him. But I want you to do me a favor. When you see him, I want you to tell him—because we looked at each other, eye to eye—I want you to tell him that he's only alive because of you."

"Daddy, are you serious? I'm not going to tell him that."

"No, really, I want you to tell him that if you see him."

He wasn't the father I once knew anymore, but he did let the kid live. He let him live, which was shocking, and it was because I asked him.

I did tell Tommy the next time I saw him. He said, "Oh, gee. Thanks." He didn't really know what to say.

Then on May 22, 1992, my father, Larry and Jimmy drove to the Brooklyn house of Lorenzo

"Larry" Lampasi. They waited until he came out of his house. He opened the gate, got in his car and backed out. When Lampasi got out of the car to go close the gate, my father stuck his rifle out the window and shot him. Jimmy started to drive away, but my father told him to stop because he wasn't sure if Lampasi was dead. Then they got out and shot him again, to be sure.

Thinking back, I realize the disease was fueling my father. That's why he was so crazy and was driving the family cars, instead of stealing cars, when he went to shoot people. Would he have done that if he was in the right frame of mind? No, never. My father was a very calculating person. He always planned things, day by day, minute by minute. But none of that was planned. As far as my father was concerned, nothing or nobody was going to stop him—not the cops, not the feds, not the other families. No one was going to stop him—ever.

That was how it was, living with my father during the war.

CHAPTER 13

DO THEY THINK I'M FUCKIN' SLEEPING?

In March 1992, the Brooklyn district attorney's office obtained a warrant for my father's arrest on a gun possession charge after two police officers saw him drop a gun out of his car window.

On March 3, the FBI closed my father as an informant because they believed that he was involved in planning violent criminal activity. Lin DeVecchio, however, adamantly denied that fact. At the beginning of April, Lin started the process to get my father reopened. He was officially reopened on April 22.

During that summer Special Agent Christopher Favo became very suspicious of Lin, thinking he was involved in some kind of misconduct that could disrupt ongoing investigations at that time. So Favo started withholding from Lin any information that had to do with my father.

It was at that time that my father's lawsuit against

Victory Memorial Hospital and his surgeon was settled after a three-week hearing. My brother and I knew he was suing the hospital, but my parents told us it was because the doctor had left scissors or some type of instrument inside my father.

One day I was lying on the couch when the phone rang. It was my father.

"I have to tell you something. There are going to be a lot of reporters coming to the house. They'll probably be there any second."

"What's going on? What's wrong?"

"I really didn't tell you the truth about what's wrong with me. I don't want you to hear it from the reporters. I want you to hear it from me."

"Okay. What's wrong?"

"I have AIDS. I got HIV from the blood transfusion and that's what the trial was about."

I was in shock, but I was trying to comfort him. I could hear in his voice how shaken up he was. I wasn't thinking about my feelings.

"Don't worry. It's okay. You'll get through this. We'll get through this."

I didn't know what to say. I really didn't know a lot about AIDS back then. I didn't freak out about it, though. It was more about comforting him, and feeling sorry that he had this disease. I wasn't thinking about anyone else, or the consequences of living with someone with AIDS. That didn't come into my head at all at first. My initial reaction was to comfort him and to tell him that it was okay. He would fight it and everything would be all right.

Then, later on, I started thinking about it and

reading up on it. I was afraid then. After that, I was worried about my son. Then other things that had happened with my father started to make sense.

After he got sick, my father used to tell me not to use his razor. He said his bathroom was his bathroom. I always used to go into his bathroom and use his razor if I didn't have one. He never said anything about it before. So even though he told me not to use his razor, I still did.

One day he saw me in his bathroom using his razor and he freaked out.

"I told you not to use my stuff."

When he shaved, he cut himself all the time and bled a lot. And I was using his razor and not knowing he had AIDS. Why didn't my parents just tell us the truth? There were always secrets. But the things that should have been secret weren't.

When my father came home after he made that call to tell me that he had AIDS, he was very emotional. He came over to me and was hugging and kissing me and crying.

"I didn't want you to feel like you had to be afraid of me," he said.

"Don't worry, Dad. I love you."

I was crying for him, not for me. I just kept thinking that I hoped he wasn't going to die. I didn't really care about me as usual. It was always him. I always put him ahead of my feelings. I always tried to protect him.

My father said he didn't tell us sooner because he didn't want us to treat him differently. He was afraid we wouldn't want to touch him or go near him.

I didn't want him to feel different. He was still the same. He was still my father. I didn't care that he had AIDS. We would get through it. I kept telling him he was strong and he was going to fight this disease.

That's what I told him—but the truth was, after I found out, I was afraid. I tried not to treat him differently, but I felt that he was testing us. When we were growing up, my father would cut fruit at night and we never thought anything of taking something from his fork.

When he was sick, he still did it and wanted us to take the fruit from his fork. I took it because I always put his feelings before mine. It was an unconditional love, but I was afraid.

In August 1992, my father, who was pretty sick by this time, arranged to turn himself in on the gun charge from March. My father called Lin and asked what was going to happen in court. My mother knows what happened.

Lin DeVecchio told Greg not to worry about it. He said, "You're going to pay a fine and then you're going to get right back out." So I went to court with Greg. But when we got there, I saw agents all over the courtroom. So I called Lin.

"What's going on? Are you sure they're going to let Greg out? There are agents all over the courtroom."

"I don't know what's going on," he said. "What do you mean, 'There are agents all over the courtroom'?"

"This place is filled with agents everywhere. Are

they going to rearrest him? Are they arresting him for something else?"

"I have no idea what's going on."

My father was rearrested that day in the courtroom for three murders, including the murder of Larry Lampasi. But Lin didn't know that was going to happen, because the FBI wasn't telling him anything.

Ultimately my father was so sick from AIDS that he was put on house arrest while he was awaiting trial for the murders. At that time we were living in the two-family on Eighty-Second Street. One of my aunts lived downstairs.

When my father was on house arrest, the tension was high in the house. He was trapped with an ankle bracelet on, which made it extra hard for us. Our once-loving, playful father was now being treated like a caged animal. He was suffering from AIDS and was on so many different medications. Some of them altered his moods, so we had to watch what we said. He would get enraged by our words if we said something wrong.

My mother told me that his doctor said he was suffering from dementia, which was a part of the later stages of AIDS. The doctor said he was dangerous—even to us. He was so bad that his doctor wanted to put him in a hospital. My mother tried to convince him to go, but he said he wanted to be home for the holidays. He was not going to the hospital, and that was it.

I was having a hard time believing what the doctors were saying. One day I went into my father's bedroom—he was putting on his socks—and I told him what my mother said.

"Well, nobody said that to me. That's news to me. So, what did they say? Did they say that I'm going crazy?"

"I don't know, Dad. I don't know what it means. I don't think you're crazy."

I didn't think that he was acting crazy at that time. He did want to go out and kill, but he couldn't. So he was trying to keep his rage to a minimum.

But for my brother, my mother and me, we had to keep things in the house as calm as possible. That was hard, though, because there were two little kids—my son and Joey's daughter—running around the house and making a mess. It was hard for him to be stuck in the house like that, under those conditions.

The disease was making him crazy and it even affected the way he treated me.

It was a little before Christmas that year and we were decorating the tree, but we couldn't find the lights. My mother told me to go to the store to get some lights.

"Why do I have to go to the store and get the lights?"

"Just go to the store and get lights. What's the big deal?"

"Linda, go get the lights," my father said.

"Okay, Dad. I'll get the lights." By the time I got back from the store, the tree was all decorated with ornaments and lights. I was pissed.

"What the fuck? You made me go to the store, and the fucking tree is decorated? What are you, fucking nuts?"

I always spoke that way and my father never cared before. That time he looked at me like he was ready to kill me. My father's friend, Louie, was at the house fixing our fish tank. My father had a fish tank put in the house because he found it relaxing to watch the fish.

My father charged at me with a closed fist and pounded my head. I was in shock—not just because it hurt, but because I thought he really was losing it. My father had never laid a hand on me before—ever. I was scared because he looked like he was crazed. I ran behind Louie, but he said not to put him in the middle of it—he was afraid he was going to get hit.

I screamed for my mother and she came running into the room.

"This girl, she better learn how to fucking talk," he said.

My father was reprimanding me. I was in my twenties and he was trying to teach me a lesson—a lesson he should have given me when I was fifteen.

I was really angry at him. I didn't talk to him for a couple weeks. I was afraid of the fact that he had lost control. It was scary to know that the doctors were right—he was dangerous even to us.

Right around this time my father asked me to help him make a videotape for Gregory Junior to see when he got out of jail. My father thought Gregory was going to be out after he served his twenty-year sentence for racketeering and extortion handed down in 1988.

My father knew he wasn't going to make it until Gregory got out of jail. He said he wanted Gregory to have a video message from him when he came home. He wanted to tell Gregory how he felt about him and that he was sorry for everything that had happened. My father wanted to be sure that Gregory had this video to watch, because his son wasn't going to have him alive. My father wanted Gregory to have a piece of him when he was released.

I told him we could make the video whenever he wanted to do it. But it wasn't long before everything came crashing down around us and we were never able to get it done.

As it turned out, Gregory never got out of jail. After another trial in 1998 for racketeering and murder—he was acquitted of murder—Gregory was sentenced to another forty years to life. I wished I had been able to do the video for my father, but in the end, Gregory probably wouldn't have been able to see it, anyway.

When it became public that my father had AIDS and that he didn't have long to live, people started taking advantage of him and our family.

For as long as I can remember, my father had this huge three-carat pinky ring. He said he had it appraised and it was worth $75,000. It was a perfect, flawless, clear diamond, with absolutely no hint of color. It was in a black onyx setting. I always used to stare at this ring—it was so big that it would blind you. When I told him how beautiful it was, he would try to teach me how to tell the difference between a good diamond and a bad diamond.

Before he was dying, he told my mother that he was going to make an engagement ring for her. My parents never officially got married and my mother always wanted to marry him. They were planning on getting married, but it didn't happen. He never had the chance to get divorced.

When he was sick, he took it to a guy he knew in the diamond exchange in Manhattan to have a ring made for my mother. When he came home, he told my mother he left it with his jeweler friend and he was going to pick it up in two days. My mother couldn't believe he left it there, but she couldn't say anything to him because he would get angry.

When he brought the ring home to show us, I knew immediately that something was wrong.

"Dad, this isn't the same diamond."

"What are you talking about? That's the same diamond. I brought it to my friend."

"Dad, this isn't the same diamond. I'm telling you, this diamond has color."

"What? Are you an expert now?"

"Yeah, I'm an expert on your diamond because I know I've stared at it long enough."

My father got really angry. He told me I saw the color because now it was in a yellow gold setting and it was reflecting the gold. I thought maybe he was right. He told my mother that if anything ever happened and we needed money, she should take the ring back to his friend to sell it and he'd give her the $75,000.

There came a point where we needed the money

and my mother had to bring the ring to my father's friend. He offered my mother $10,000. I screamed that he told my father it was worth $75,000. He tried to make up some story. I went ballistic in the middle of the diamond exchange. He called security to escort me out. I knew he took advantage of my father because he was sick and not thinking rationally.

Even the guys in his own crew were taking advantage of my father when it came to money or whatever they could get from him. Once his disease started progressing, and my brother was on his own, the guys out in the streets started to do things to him that they never would have done if my father was in his prime and in good health.

One day my brother told my father that two guys in his crew, "Mr. X" and "Mr. Y," were chasing him. They had guns and they were going to kill him. My father didn't believe what Joey was saying.

"What? Are you crazy? They would never do that. They're with me. They would never chase you. What are you taking? You're paranoid."

My brother was really pissed.

"You're in on it. If you don't believe me, then . . ."

My brother was accusing my father of knowing about it because my father wasn't believing him. My mother asked me what kind of drugs my brother was on. I told her I didn't really know, but I knew he was doing something.

So my brother went upstairs and locked himself in his room—we were both separated from our spouses and living at home. Joey married young and had a kid right away. I went upstairs to talk to him.

"Joe, what's going on?"

"They were chasing me. They want to kill me. Daddy's in on it. I know it."

"Joe, are you sure that they were chasing you? Are you positive?"

"Linda, what am I stupid? I may be fucked up right now, but I know that they were chasing me. They were chasing me with guns, and they want to kill me. I got away from them."

My brother was very scared; he wouldn't leave the house for weeks. My father had to call Mr. X and Mr. Y to the house. He asked them what was going on. They said they didn't have any idea what my brother was talking about. My father called my brother downstairs and they tried to make my brother out to be a psycho, like he was sick. They told him they'd get him help.

Meanwhile my brother was flipping out.

"You're a fucking liar. You did this."

Nobody believed him. I believed him, but I couldn't and wouldn't believe my father had anything to do with it.

My father thought that my brother was just being paranoid and hallucinating because he was doing drugs. My father was trying to talk him into getting off the stuff, while he was consoling him and telling him he would never let anyone touch him.

The more I thought about it, the more I thought maybe what my brother was saying was true. After all, Mr. X wasn't doing the right thing when it came to my father. In fact, everyone was trying to take advantage of my father. Mr. X knew that my father was suffering from AIDS and from AIDS-related dementia, so he stole $40,000 from him.

My father had given Mr. X the money for some deal, but I don't remember which one. But Mr. X told my father that the cops raided his house in the middle of the night and they took the forty grand. My father asked Lin if what Mr. X was saying was true. Lin said he was lying because Mr. X's house hadn't been raided. My father never did anything about it, though, because Mr. X is still living.

Years later, after my father and my brother were both dead, I ran into someone from the old neighborhood who was in the life. He told me that Mr. X had just been pretending to be with my father. He said Mr. X had been shying away from my father and had no loyalty to him. In reality he had been with some other guy.

Then out of nowhere he said, "Remember when Mr. X and Mr. Y were chasing your brother?"

"What are you talking about? My father said that wasn't true."

"Wasn't true? Mr. X and Mr. Y were supposed to kill your brother."

"Are you serious? That's what my brother told us."

This guy confirmed that it was true. He told me "Mr. Z," another member of my father's crew, put a hit on my brother because he found out that Joey had given his wife drugs. Mr. X and Mr. Y were supposed to do the hit for Mr. Z.

Holy shit! The whole story that my brother told me was true. Everything that my brother said to me was confirmed, although I never doubted him for one second.

Shortly after that incident happened with my brother, things went from bad to horrible.

It was December 29, 1992.

The war that had erupted inside the Colombo family in 1991 between jailed boss, Carmine Persico, and his acting boss, Vic Orena, was winding down. When all was said and done, twelve people, including three innocent bystanders, had been murdered—four by my father.

That night in December, my father was really juiced up from the AIDS drugs and the steroids. On top of everything else the street pot he was smoking really messed him up and sent him over the edge of insanity—so over the edge that he didn't even know his left eye had been blown right out of its socket.

My brother Joey came over to the house that night with his friend Joe Randazzo—they were both just twenty-one. They told my father that they had had a problem in the street with a couple Lucchese crime family drug dealers, Michael "Mikey Flattop" DeRosa and Ronald "Messy Marvin" Moran. One of them had pulled a gun on Joey and Joe.

My father was flipping out because someone actually thought he could pull a gun on his son. He was yelling and screaming in the house. His whole demeanor was different. He was enraged beyond recognition. You wouldn't even recognize him if you knew him.

"What? Do they think I'm fuckin' sleeping? They think because I'm in this house, I'm fuckin' sleeping. They think they're going to do this to my son. This ain't gonna happen to my son. They think they're gonna pull a gun on my son. Fuck that!"

When my mother heard him ranting and raving, she tried to calm him down. She told him to call

Larry Mazza the next morning. He should let Larry and the rest of the crew handle it. But because my mother was always on top of my father—when she nagged, she could drive you crazy—he just "yessed" her to death.

My mother went to bed. I was upstairs writing a letter to a friend, a member of my father's crew, who was in prison. But it was stewing in my father, and he was enraged with everything that was going on with my brother. I heard him banging stuff around. So I went downstairs and he was acting crazy— *really crazy.*

Next thing I knew, he was gone with my brother and Joe. My brother didn't want him to go, but Joe and my brother didn't have any say.

"Get in the fuckin' car," my father said. "We're going there and we're going to straighten it out."

That's what my brother thought—they were going there to straighten it out. He didn't even know my father had a gun on him.

So they left and the ankle bracelet was going off. I ran outside—it was around midnight. I was so confused. I knew that Mikey DeRosa lived on Eightieth Street, between Thirteenth and Fourteenth Avenues, closer to Thirteenth. And I was on Eighty-Second Street, between Twelfth and Thirteenth Avenues, closer to Thirteenth. We were only two short blocks away.

Then I heard gunshots and screaming; the ankle bracelet was going off. I was completely panicked. I ran back into the house. I was running back and forth. I didn't know what to do. As I was about to run back outside, the car pulled up and stopped right in front of the driveway. My father got out. He was wearing a white jacket; it was soaked in blood.

I knew my father had AIDS, but I had to help him. I didn't even have any shoes on. I grabbed my boots and threw them on, because I didn't want to get blood on my feet. I was thinking about helping my father, but I was afraid of AIDS. I went back to the front door and he was standing there covered in blood. There was blood all over his face, so I couldn't completely make out what had happened to him—yet.

I was freaking out. He went to the kitchen and sat down on a chair. He had his hand on his eye. My first instinct was to reach out and touch him. He screamed at me to leave him alone. Where was Joey? Where was my brother? My father's yelling that Joey was in the car. Then he told me to get him a towel.

As I went to get the towel, I heard my mother's footsteps on the stairs. I screamed at her not to come down. I didn't know if she was going to freak out if my brother was dead in the car. Of course, she came down. She had to.

When I gave my father the towel, he took his hand off his face and I saw that he had a bullet hole in his eye. His eyelid was closed shut, but you could see that his eye was gone. It was drooping down. He had a hole in his face, right by the corner of his eye. He was really hurt. I knew I had to call an ambulance.

"You're not calling an ambulance. I'm not hurt. I'm not hurt. I got glass in my eye. Just give me the fuckin' water. Just give me ice. Give me a fuckin' glass of scotch."

He was sitting there covered in blood, asking for water, ice and a glass of scotch. His ankle bracelet was still going off. The phone was ringing. My father told me to answer it.

"Hello."

"There's a problem with the bracelet."

"Yeah, I don't know what happened. Hold on a second, here's my father."

He got on the phone with them, all calm and nonchalant, and told them everything was all right.

"Everything's fine. There's no problem. I don't know what's going on with this thing. It's just beepin'. I'm sitting right here. I answered your fuckin' call."

I couldn't take it anymore. I told my mother to take care of my father. I had to go to the car, so I ran outside. My brother wasn't in the car, but his friend Joe was in the backseat, gurgling from his mouth. The car was covered in blood, and I didn't have anything on my hands. I ran back up to the house.

"Dad, Joey's not in the car!" I screamed. "Joey's not in the car!"

"He's in the fucking car." He still thought my brother was in the car.

Oh, my God, where was my brother? My brother was dead. He was on the street somewhere fucking dead. I was really panicking. I ran back inside and called Joe Fish for some reason. I hated Joe Fish. He didn't answer, so I left him a message.

"You fucking rat bastard, you don't answer the fucking phone." Then I hung up on him and called Larry. I told him to get to the house right then to take my father to the hospital because he'd been shot and I didn't know where Joey was. I didn't know if he was dead or alive. And Joe Randazzo was in the backseat of the car, bleeding to death.

I ran back outside and the twin girls from across the street came running over. They had heard all the commotion from me freaking out. I told them to get me gloves. Gloves for cleaning, gloves for the winter, I didn't care. And I told them to call an ambulance.

One of them ran to her house and got me rubber cleaning gloves and winter gloves. I put them both on my hands. I pushed the front seat forward so there was more room in the back. But I was afraid to move Joe. I wanted to grab him and I wanted to hold him, because I knew he was going to die. But what if he wasn't going to die? He had a head wound and I didn't want to touch him and hurt him more.

So I talked to him. I tried to comfort him. I didn't know if he could hear me, but he was making sounds and maybe he could hear me.

"Joe, everything's going to be okay. The ambulance is coming. It's Linda. It's your little sister. You're going to be okay." I was twenty-three then and a few years older than Joe Randazzo. But ever since I could remember, he used to tease me and call me his "little sister."

While that was happening, Larry had come to take my father to the hospital. My father was completely oblivious to everything that was going on. He still thought Joey was in the car. He still thought he had glass in his eye. He didn't have a clue what had happened to him. He was already suffering from AIDS-induced dementia, but now he was completely demented.

I loved my father. I cared about my father. But he had lost so much control, I thought he was going to die that night. I almost prayed that he would. I prayed that God would take him out of this hell that his life had become. He was suffering from a horrible disease—a disease that took away all of his rationality. Dementia was settling in and taking over. I felt it would be best if he passed that night, because his suffering would end.

I wanted my father to live forever. To me, he was my world. He was invincible. That wasn't the case anymore, though. But at that moment, I wasn't concerned about him. I knew Larry was taking him to the hospital. I was scared to death for my brother.

Where was my brother? I didn't know where he was. And I knew I had to stay with Joe. Then the ambulance came and the EMTs were pushing me away from him.

"Please help him!" I was screaming. "Please tell me if he's going to be okay. Is he going to live?"

They got me out of the way so they could do their work. They said he had a serious head trauma and they didn't know what was going to happen. I moved back and let them do what they had to do. Then they took him away and all I could see were those flashing lights from the ambulance.

To this day I can't look at the lights of an ambulance because it takes me immediately back to that night. I get an instant flashback to that whole scene of Joe in the backseat of the car. It's sick. It's like a trauma—a scar that will never heal.

The lights were going everywhere. There was blood everywhere. I had blood all over the gloves on my hands. The car smelled of blood—my father's blood and Joe Randazzo's blood—and death. It was disgusting. The whole scene was a nightmare.

The ambulance left and I was standing outside, frozen. I was so in shock. I didn't know what to do. Where was my brother? I heard another ambulance in the vicinity of Eightieth Street. Was my brother there? I was about to start running to Eightieth, when a car service car pulled up and my brother got out.

He looked at me, and I looked at him. He opened his mouth to say something, but all that came out were sobs—deep, gut-wrenching sobs. All I could say was "Oh, my God, Joey."

"Lin, you don't even know what happened." His face went slack; his mouth was slightly open. I could see the color draining from his face. He was shaking—he couldn't stop shaking—and he couldn't catch his breath.

"Joe, listen, they're alive."

"They are?"

"Yeah, Daddy went to the hospital, and Joe just went to the hospital, too. They're both alive right now."

"Joe can't be alive. He got shot in the head, Lin. You don't know what Daddy did. He made like he was going to shake Mike's hand, and he did—he shook his hand—and I thought everything was squashed. I thought we were going to, you know, walk away, and everything was settled. I thought we were going to drive away."

My brother was so distraught. He had just witnessed his friend get shot in the head, and he thought he was going to get killed, too.

"Daddy told Mike to make his friends go inside. But Mike just told them to step aside—you know, to move down. He says, 'Guys, move down there. I'm gonna talk to him by myself.' That was crazy for him to do, but he trusted Daddy. Lin, Daddy shook his hand. I thought it was squashed. Next thing I know, Mike goes to walk away and Daddy shoots him. And they start shooting back. A bullet went through Daddy's nose and took out his eye. When I turned around to tell Joe to duck, he got shot in the head. He can't be alive."

He was coughing and gasping and crying. The deep, rumbling sobs tore through his chest. He had this wild look in his eyes, which scared the shit out of me.

"Joe is alive. He is. They took him to the hospital."

"Lin, I blacked out. I put my arm up to protect my head and a bullet grazed my arm."

Joey held his arm up and I could see the skid mark of a bullet. It looked just like a tire tread. I grabbed his hand and dragged him into my aunt's apartment. I didn't want to bring him into our house because the cops could come because of my father. But they'd have to get a warrant to search her place. As soon as he could, Joey called his wife, Maria, to come to the house.

Maria was hysterical when she arrived, but she was trying to calm him down. Joey was sitting on the floor and she sat down next to him. Holding him. Crying with him. They were both in shock.

Maybe an hour later, the cops showed up at my door. I asked what they wanted. They told me it was a crime scene and they had to come in to search. I told them there was no crime scene in my house. They insisted there was. We went back and forth like that a couple times. Finally I asked if they had a warrant. When they said no, I told them the only way they were getting into the house was when they had a warrant. But they weren't giving up so easy.

"You know, there's a car in front of your house full of blood, and an ambulance was here that took a body, and you're telling me this isn't a crime scene?"

"The crime scene is outside. The crime scene is not inside. So when you have a warrant, you can come in my house."

"We just need to come in and talk to you," one cop said.

"Fine, you can come in and talk, but you're not searching my house."

"So, where's your father?" the cop said, looking around.

"I don't know."

"Well, did he come home?"

"Listen, all I know is this—something happened, some crazy shit. . . . These guys came to the house and took my father. I don't know who they were. I don't know where they took him."

"Did you recognize them?"

"No. I have no clue. They came here, they took him out of the house, there was nothing I could do about it and my father left with them."

I made up some crazy story. They must have thought that I was nuts. I didn't want to tell them that he went to the hospital, because I thought he was going to die, and I wanted him to die in peace. They could figure it out on their own.

"Where's your brother?"

"I don't know where my brother is. I don't know what's happening."

While this was happening, my mother was walking around like a zombie. They couldn't talk to her—she was completely shut down. In shock. I wasn't going to let them talk to her, anyway. I was like the boss at that point.

That's the way it always was. When there were serious situations, I took over. If my father wasn't around, I took over. They weren't going to talk to my mother. They weren't going to talk to anyone but me.

Finally the cops gave up and left.

Almost right after the cops left, Larry called from Mount Sinai Hospital. He said my father was going to have surgery so the doctors could remove his eyeball from the socket. They couldn't repair it. His eyeball was still in there, but it had been blown up. I wasn't happy to hear that news. If my father lived, he would be living the rest of his life suffering and dying in a prison somewhere. Plus he was only going to have one eye. He'd be in a hospital or a jail and he'd live a really tortured life, dying in prison without his family.

My mother went to the hospital that night to see my father. I didn't go right away. I stayed home to comfort Joey. He was inconsolable.

When my mother got to the hospital, my father was in the emergency room. The marshals who were there wouldn't let her see him. Then they searched her and decided she could see him if she wanted, but she decided to wait in the waiting room. He hadn't gone into surgery yet and she didn't want to see him with his eye shot out.

While she was waiting, the marshals called and told her my father wanted to see her.

"I went to the room he was in. He was sitting there, all bandaged. When I looked at him, I got dizzy. It was shocking. It's something I can't even describe. There I am dying, but he had a smile on his face, and he said, 'That's all right, sweetheart. You can call me "One-eyed Greg" now.' Because he always tried to make us feel better, no matter what the situation was. He always tried to make like it was nothing—like it wasn't a big deal," my mother said.

The next morning, at about six-thirty, the cops came back with their warrant. I was getting ready to go to the hospital. They had their warrant, so I had to let them in. But it didn't matter, because my mother had cleaned up all the blood, and I knew that there was nothing in the house that they wanted. They were looking for the gun my father used to shoot Mikey DeRosa.

I didn't care that the cops were in the house. I just cared about seeing Joe Randazzo. I wanted to know what happened at the hospital and if he was going to be okay.

When I walked into his room, I knew it wasn't looking good for him. I remember seeing him in that bed. I can still see his face now—his head was all wrapped up. I just knew that there was no way he was going survive. If he did live, he was going to be a vegetable.

His family wanted to know who was with Joe in the car. I told them I helped Joe until the ambulance came. Once they found out who I was, and exactly what had happened that night, they turned on me.

They kicked me out of Joe's room. They told me not to come back. They didn't want me there.

Although I was devastated, I understood. They blamed my family. I wanted to be by Joe's side, but it wasn't really my place. I respected the family's wishes. How could I not? He died the next day.

I didn't see my father that day. I went to the hospital with my mother a couple days later. He wasn't supposed to have visitors, but his lawyer snuck us in and arranged for us to see him in the atrium. I was sitting there and he was telling us everything was going to be okay. I was traumatized. I just remember seeing him and feeling afraid because he didn't have an eye.

My brother went into a really bad state of depression. Joey decided to stay at my parents for a while. I was living there as well. He just basically locked himself in his room and stayed there. He didn't know how to deal with what had happened. He didn't want people to see him cry.

Joey felt really guilty. He had so much guilt that Joe died and he lived. He was in shock. He was angry at my father because he thought they were going to see Mikey DeRosa to straighten things out. It wasn't supposed to happen the way it did. At the same time, he was still his father.

My brother just stayed in that room. He wasn't leaving my mother—he needed my mother. The problem was, my mother wasn't dealing with things much better than Joey. She just completely zoned out and was like a robot. She just went with whatever was happening and did whatever she felt she was supposed to do.

As for Mikey DeRosa—he lived and went back into the streets. The shooting actually gave him rank out in the streets, because he was the guy who shot Greg Scarpa. He was the one who got Greg Scarpa—him and his crew.

I ran into Mikey recently and he told me his side of the story about what had happened that night. He told me it all started because a guy who was working for my brother, selling drugs, borrowed money from Mikey, but he wasn't paying him back. One day Mikey saw this guy in front of his house, so Mikey pulled the money out of the guy's pocket. The guy told him it was Joey's money, but Mikey didn't care.

He said a few hours later, Joey and Joe Randazzo went to his house with baseball bats. He said they tried to hit him, so he ran inside, grabbed a gun, ran back out and started shooting at them. Joe and Joey jumped in their car and drove off, with Mikey chasing them up the block.

When they left, Mikey went back into his house and called James "Jimmy Frogs" Galione, his street boss in the Lucchese family. Jimmy told him to stay in his house. Jimmy said he was getting made and didn't want any trouble.

But when my father pulled up with Joey and Joe, Mikey's brother ran out of the house to talk to him. In the meantime Mikey gave guns to the rest of the guys who were with him. He then went over to the car and shook my father's hand.

My father asked what was going on with him and Joey. Mikey said it didn't have anything to do with Joey. It had to do with a guy who owed him money. Then my father told Joey to get out of the car. He shook Mikey's hand again, like everything was over. My father told Mikey to call his guys off, which he did.

As the guys were walking away, Mikey said he felt like he was hit with a baseball bat. The bullet went into his neck and he fell to the ground. Messy Marvin emptied his whole clip into the car, where my father and Joe Randazzo were sitting. Joe got hit in the back of the head.

Mikey got up and started to run. My father shot at him again; this time the bullet hit him in the back and another bullet got him in the side. He said when my father was shot, the bullet went through his nose and came out the side of his face, taking his eye with it.

He said my brother was lucky because he had been out of the car and left when the shooting started. Mikey somehow made it back into his house. He was very happy because he thought my father was dead. As he was making a phone call, he looked up. He said, "What the fuck! The guy just drove away with a hole in his eye."

Because of the shoot-out and the fact that he had shot my father, Mikey's stature in the Lucchese family was escalated and he was making more money. Mikey and Messy Marvin were then on record with the Lucchese family, and everybody knew they were protected.

They say there's three sides to every story. In this case there's my brother's side, Mikey's side and the truth. And I believe my brother's side to be the truth.

CHAPTER 14

THE BEGINNING OF THE END

While my father was in the hospital, the prosecutors revoked his house arrest. When he left Mount Sinai Hospital, the marshals took him to the Metropolitan Correctional Center (MCC) in Manhattan.

My mother went to visit him and was horrified at what she saw.

"I noticed his skin was turning purple and black. So I got in touch with his AIDS doctor, Dr. Jeffrey Gumprecht, on Park Avenue and I told him what was happening. He got in touch with the doctor at MCC and they brought him to another hospital. He was bleeding internally. That's why he was so purple," my mother said.

When my mother got to the hospital, the marshals were standing at the door to his room. They had him handcuffed to the bed.

"I asked them if they could please take off the

handcuffs. 'Where's he going?' I wanted to know. So they took off the handcuffs and they let me stay with him. Some days I'd bring him food and they didn't mind. So I'd stay with him all day in the hospital," my mother recalled.

After he was released from the hospital, they brought him back to MCC, and then he went to court. Because my father had violated the terms of his house arrest, the judge revoked his bail in January and he went back to MCC.

Shortly after that, he was indicted for racketeering and three murders, in addition to the gun charges and murder conspiracy he had originally been charged with. He was arraigned on February 18, 1993. He pleaded not guilty and tried to get out on bail again.

Dr. Gumprecht, who had been treating my father since 1990, explained to Judge Jack Weinstein about my father's condition. He told him that my father only had a month or two to live. The doctor said that my father had gotten worse since he had been sent to MCC and had lost twenty-five pounds. He called it "AIDS wasting" and said my father was losing more weight.

The doctor told the judge that my father was also losing weight because he had lost his stomach in 1986 because of a bleeding ulcer. And that meant he had to have a special diet and needed to be fed frequently—something the doctor said MCC couldn't provide.

And if that wasn't bad enough, the doctor told the judge about the gunshot that destroyed my father's left eye and part of his face, and now there was only soft tissue left between his skin and brain. My father also had an infection on his face that was probably going to spread to his brain and he needed to have intravenous antibiotics almost immediately. He explained to the judge that my father was also suffering from AIDS-related dementia and didn't have a firm grasp on reality.

The doctor said my father had trouble walking and standing and had fallen a few times at MCC, putting other inmates, who had volunteered to help him, at risk because he would bleed. The doctor said my father needed basic nursing care, which wasn't available at MCC. Not only that, he said if my father contracted tuberculosis or the flu—both were prevalent at MCC—he would probably die. Dr. Gumprecht said my father needed to be in a hospital with AIDS specialists who would be able to treat him.

The government didn't offer any medical testimony but relied on evidence before the judge that MCC could give my father adequate medical care.

The judge agreed that the medical facilities at MCC were not that great. But Judge Weinstein said that Beekman Hospital, located in Manhattan, had an agreement with MCC and treated inmates who needed to be hospitalized.

The judge acknowledged that although the federal prison system had full hospital facilities and could take care of my father, they were far away from New York. That meant we wouldn't be able to visit him, and his doctor wouldn't be able to treat him. Judge Weinstein said if my father was sent to a federal prison that was far from New York, he'd continue to suffer a rapid decline in prison without "humane care in the last days of his life."

But even though he was so sick, the judge said, my father would most likely commit more crimes if he was allowed to go free. So, on February 19, 1993, the judge decided to send my father to Beekman Hospital under certain conditions, including that he would be guarded 24/7 by U.S. Marshals and my mother would pay for the marshals, as well as for his medical care.

A few days later the hospital told the judge that the infection on my father's face had cleared up and he didn't have to be in the hospital any longer, so the marshals brought him back to MCC. Then my father asked to be admitted to Cabrini Hospice. He said a bed was being held for him.

The government didn't want him to go to the hospice, saying MCC could deal with his medical needs. Judge Weinstein said that was probably true when it came to his physical illnesses, but MCC wouldn't be able to handle his psychological and emotional problems or do anything to help our family's suffering.

The judge said the Cabrini program, on the other hand, was designed to ease the distress of the patient and the family—things the court should take into consideration.

"It must be emphasized that the defendant is still presumed to be innocent. He is deprived of his liberty, only to prevent his flight and danger to the community," Judge Weinstein said. "Both of these problems can be solved by having guards constantly posted at the expense of defendant's family."

My mother had something to do with the judge's decision to send my father to hospice: "I told the judge—with the doctor—that he only had a few months to live. Then the judge called me up and said, 'You know, you're responsible if anything happens.' I said, 'He'll be fine.' So in March, he was put under guard in the Cabrini Hospice. And I had to pay for it—two U.S. Marshals to guard him twenty-four hours a day, seven days a week, at fifteen dollars an hour each.

"I used to go down and get liquor and food for him and the marshals—they were all eating. And I'd get cookies and other food for the other patients. There were young guys there with AIDS and they were in bad shape. Greg was always worried about everybody. He'd tell me, 'Go see if that kid wants anything' or 'Go see if this one wants anything.' There was food and liquor, and he enjoyed it. He was there six weeks. But I looked like the patient, not him, because I was there twenty-four/seven. He looked great."

Then after six weeks, my father told my mother that maybe he should go to Rikers Island.

"So after I spent fifty thousand dollars, he decided he'd go to Rikers, because Dr. Gumprecht said he knew the AIDS doctor at Rikers and he would be put in that unit. So that's where he ended up going. Greg made friends with the doctor over there, and the doctor took care of him. And Greg stayed there until he was sentenced in December 1993," my mother explained.

The last time I saw my father, he was in Rikers. It was a horrible place. They made it so hard to visit. It was a nightmare. I hated seeing him there, and I was horrified when I left and had to leave him there.

It was different when he was in the hospice. Even

though he was guarded by the marshals, it was still a relaxed atmosphere. I knew it wasn't difficult to leave and then go back the next day because it was more of a homelike setting.

So I didn't visit him that much when he was in Rikers. That was really hard because I never went a day without telling him I loved him. I didn't want to see him deteriorating behind the prison walls. I just couldn't face it.

Maybe if the disease had progressed more slowly, I would have been able to deal with it better. But knowing he was suffering so badly in prison, I just couldn't go there, see him and leave. It was also a defense mechanism. I had to protect myself, which sounds selfish, but it really wasn't selfish because I had a kid to take care of.

In May 1993, my father pleaded guilty to three murders—Vincent Fusaro, Nicholas "Nicky Black" Grancio, and Lorenzo "Larry" Lampasi—and several counts of conspiracy to commit murder. He was sentenced on December 15, 1993. He thought he was going home because he was so sick, but that didn't happen.

Initially he was sentenced to life in prison, which was later reduced to ten years by Judge Weinstein, who cited "humanitarian reasons" for his decision to lessen the original sentence. Shortly after being sentenced, he was transferred from Rikers to a federal prison hospital near Pittsburgh.

My mother used to visit him there: "I used to meet him in the place near Pittsburgh. That's where they sent him because they said he couldn't stay at Rikers. He went to court, and the judge said he was going to keep him close. Yeah, right, thanks—that was pretty far. I don't remember exactly where it was, but I took a plane to Pittsburgh and then took a little six-seater plane to the town the prison was in."

When my mother got to the prison hospital in Pennsylvania, she went crazy because of the way they had been treating my father.

"His hair was down to his shoulders, his nails were not cut, he wasn't shaved—I went nuts. I flipped out on the people in charge. He told me he was sleeping on this hard bed. I said, 'Get me a scissors—are you afraid to cut his hair? I'll do it.' They said they'd have someone come down and do it," my mother stated.

"I said, 'This should've been done—look what he looks like.' I was hysterical. And then they sent some-body down. I said, 'You're discriminating against him because he has AIDS, and I'm reporting you. You're not letting him in the general population, where he's supposed to be. You can't discriminate against him because he has AIDS. And you just can't keep him locked in the room.' The marshals were with us all the time, but I didn't give a shit. I mean, God, they didn't do anything for him there," she continued.

So my mother contacted the right people, who convinced the authorities to move him to the Federal Medical Center (FMC) in Rochester, Minnesota: "I got in touch with Greg's doctor and the AIDS ac-tivists. They talked to the prison people and then they moved him to Rochester, Minnesota. They moved him because they couldn't do anything for him in the other place."

When they moved him to Minnesota, my mother

had to take a plane to Minneapolis–Saint Paul, and from there she took another plane to Rochester. The medical center for prisoners was right near the Mayo Clinic, which was one of the local hospitals that worked closely with FMC Rochester.

"I used to leave on a Friday morning, about five, to make the early flight to get there for the eight a.m. visit, every week. I'd stay until Monday and leave after that day's visit. Then I'd go back again on Friday," my mother shared. "I used to put him in the wheelchair, and I'd tell the staff to give me a jacket because I was going to take him outside for a cigarette and a walk. Of course, the marshals followed us when we went outside. I'd take him for a walk and buy him food from the vending machines. He was like eighty pounds. He loved it when we went outside. He used to put his head up in the sun and say, 'Oh, I feel like I'm in Florida.' Sometimes he was in his right mind, sometimes he wasn't."

Then, all of a sudden, my mother said the prisoners somehow found out that he had AIDS: "He cut himself in the visiting room and people complained. So then they told me I couldn't take him to the visitors' room anymore. They said he had to stay in his room, but they still let me take him outside for a walk. But he was pretty bad, anyway. He wasn't eating, so I used to force-feed him. I'd tell the staff to get me fresh fruit. They'd give me some fresh fruit, like oranges. So I'd squeeze the oranges and give him that—at least he could drink that."

I never went to see my father in Rochester. I was trying to get all the paperwork done so I could visit, but it didn't get done in time. My brother went once, but he couldn't go again. He didn't want to see him like that. But my mother said my father would ask about Joey.

"Greg kept asking for my son. One day he was lying in bed, and he says, 'I thought Joey was coming up.' I'd tell him Joey was sick with a strep throat. Then the next week, he'd ask, 'Where's Joey?' And I'd say he was still sick. But Joey couldn't see him like that. Joey went once, and he flipped out. He just couldn't stop crying. Joey couldn't deal with it. I couldn't deal with it, either," my mother recounted. "But if I didn't go . . . I had to go. But it was a horrible sight. It was better that the kids didn't see him that way. It was a terrible sight. He had sores all over his body, in his mouth, everywhere. He was about fifty pounds because he couldn't eat.

"One day, Greg was in bed—and he only had the one eye—I saw a tear coming down the eye. I asked why he was crying. He said, 'I can't believe what happened. I can't believe what I did to you and the kids.' I said, 'Oh, Greg. Don't worry. You're coming home.' But he knew he wasn't. He said, 'You know, I wanted to retire.' He did want to retire until the war started. He really wanted to get out of it. He wanted to go to Florida and stay there. He didn't want to be involved in it anymore. It was just too much. He never mentioned God, though. He just said that he was sorry for what he did—for what he did to us. For making us suffer. For whatever suffering we did.

"He never said he was sorry for killing anyone, except Tommy Amato, who he killed by accident, and Joe Brewster. Those were the only regrets he really had of the people he murdered," my mother concluded. "The others—they tried to kill him. And after they tried to kill him when Linda and her kid were in the other car, he'd have killed anybody. He just got crazy. He wanted to kill anybody that was involved—and he did get a few."

Even though my father was so sick at Rochester, he always asked my mother how Joey and I were doing and how my son and Joey's daughter were doing. The only picture he had on the wall in his room was a picture of my son. He would look at it every day.

"When we were sitting in his room, he'd take my hand and ask how the kids were and how our grandson and granddaughter were. He loved them. Then he'd ask, 'Everything all right with money?' I'd say yeah, but it really wasn't. I didn't want to tell him that everybody took the money, because he'd probably escape. He probably would have," my mother said.

I didn't get to see my father before he died, but at least my mother was there to celebrate his last birthday with him: "His birthday was May eighth, so I got him a piece of cake. Then I told one of the nurses and she said we would all go into his room and sing 'Happy Birthday' to him. So we did and he was all smiles. I was trying to get him home because he didn't have very long to live. I got his doctor on it, I got those AIDS people—everybody was on it.

"About a month after his birthday I was visiting Greg and I got a call from the doctor who said because Greg was bedridden and couldn't move, the judge was going to allow him to go home. But then I got another call and the doctor said he couldn't come home. He said the prosecutor had called him and asked if Greg could move the finger he pulled the trigger with, and the doctor said he could move it. So I asked if he told the DA that Greg only weighed, like, fifty pounds. The doctor said he did tell him that. The prosecutor was worried that Greg would go out and kill somebody if he was allowed to go home. I said, 'You have to be kidding me.' But I thought that if he did go home, he probably would have killed someone.

"That day I tried to take Greg for a walk, but he didn't want to go. He didn't want to do anything. He just wanted to lie there and hold my hand, and that's what we did. I left that day. The next morning I got a phone call that he had passed," my mother shared.

The day my father died—it was June 8, 1994— I talked to him on the phone. I told him I was going to see him that weekend. I was just waiting for the papers, which were supposed to arrive that day.

"I don't know if I can wait that long," he said.

"Dad, please, I'm coming this weekend." He told my mother that it was going to be over very soon, and it was. He didn't make it to the weekend. He knew he was dying—I guess that was his last phone call.

That same morning I called my mother and told her that I had just gotten the papers so that I could visit him. But it was too late.

When my mother told me that he had died, the feeling of loss was so tremendous that I didn't know how I was going to make it through it. I felt guilty that I hadn't gone to see him before he died, but I couldn't face it.

When he was arrested and he was no longer accessible to us, and we weren't accessible to him and able to be there for him, that was a very painful time in my life. I wasn't protecting myself by not visiting him, I was in too much pain to watch this person I loved so much—my hero, my father, my life—suffer. I couldn't bear the fact that he would be in that prison and not being able to take care of him, knowing that he was living with the guilt of what he had done to us.

My father was my best friend. I went to him before I went to anyone else. I wasn't able to see him because the bond that we had was so unbelievably strong that when that bond was broken because we had no choice, it was as if my lifeline had been taken away. My best friend had been taken away.

I thought about all the times when I was a kid and I told my father that I hated him, and I felt so bad because I never hated him—not for one second.

I hated what was happening to our family, but I never hated him. I always loved my father, no matter what, even if I was angry with him. Hate was never something that I ever felt, although I used the word. I hated who he became, but it wasn't his fault—it was the disease.

It was more being angry because deep down I knew that this was going to be the end of our family as we knew it from when we were kids. I knew it wasn't going to end in a good way, and I said that to my father many times. I hated that life and I hated the fact that I had to lose him.

After my father died, the prison officials said they were going to send him home on a plane. I didn't want him to be alone, so I went to the funeral parlor and waited in the front for his body to arrive.

I waited there all night. I called my mother every hour on the hour, asking where he was. I didn't have a cell phone. I had to go to a pay phone. At seven-thirty in the morning I started banging on the door until the funeral director opened it.

"My father, Greg Scarpa, was supposed to come here last night. Where is he?"

"He's here. We bring the bodies in through a separate door."

"Well, I'm his daughter. I want to see him."

"We can't really let you see him, because we just got him. We don't know what condition he's in right now and we have to prep him."

"Well, can I still be in the room with him? If he's in the coffin they sent him in, can I stay with him?"

"Sure, no problem."

So I went into the room, and the guy walked away. I shut the doors, and I figured out how to open the coffin. At first, I just opened it about an inch, and then I got scared, and I closed it. But then I didn't even care what I was going to see. I just wanted my father.

I opened the coffin all the way, and I put half my body on top of him—I leaned my head and my chest on his chest and I started to cry. I was so distraught when I saw him. It disturbs me now even to think about it. Then I softly sang the song to him that we danced to at my wedding reception—"Wind Beneath My Wings." That song had a lot of meaning for us because he was my hero.

Then the funeral director walked in, and he flipped out.

"Oh, my God. What did you do?"

I just glared at him. "Get out and leave me alone with my father."

The guy was absolutely beside himself, but he just turned around and walked out of the room.

I was able to be strong and deal with my father's death. Once I saw him, it was a relief, even though I knew that he was gone. I broke down afterward.

When my father died, his role as a government informer was an open secret. As a result his funeral was mainly attended by relatives. There was no lavish Mafia funeral for Gregory Scarpa Senior.

CHAPTER 15

THEY KILLED
YOUR BROTHER

After my father died, my brother went into a downward spiral. He became very depressed and kind of lost.

My brother missed my father badly. He was heart-broken. He used to tell me, "Life's not the same without Dad."

We used to tell each other that we were afraid to be happy. Whenever we were happy, something bad would happen. A couple months after my father died, Joey asked me if I could see myself old.

"No, not really. Could you?"

"No, I don't see myself old at all, ever."

Even though Joey and I were only two years apart, we never hung out together. He had his friends, and I had mine. It wasn't until we were both married and going through tough times in our marriages that we started to get closer.

One day he called me. He had just bought a beautiful, flashy red car. He said, "I'm picking you up and taking you for a ride. You ready?" I said I was ready. So he picked me up and we went for a ride. He blasted Pearl Jam on the radio. I couldn't believe I didn't know that about him.

"You like Pearl Jam?"

"This is what I listen to."

"I thought you were more of a disco guy."

"I like that, too, but I listen to Pearl Jam. I love Pearl Jam."

I thought that was pretty cool. I was in the passenger seat of my little brother's car, and we're blasting the radio to Pearl Jam. It was nice.

Joey tried to get away after my father died. Lin DeVecchio told us to keep him out of Brooklyn. He told my mother he would pay for everything to send him and the family to Florida. Joey went to Florida, but he missed his daughter. He called my mother the next night and asked her to go down there. She flew there the next morning and stayed a few days with him.

When she went back to New York, he kept calling her because he wanted to come home. He came back because he didn't want people to think he was running away because his father wasn't around to protect him anymore.

When he got back, my brother started hanging out in the Brooklyn neighborhoods. He was looking for ways to make some fast money. He was separated from his wife and had to pay child support.

One of the people Joey started hanging out with was Vinny Rizzuto. They weren't best friends. Instead, it was more about making some scores. A Brooklyn drug dealer told Joey how he could make a quick buck by buying and then selling some cheap pot. Joey gave that information to Vinny. But instead of buying the pot, Vinny, Joey and Joey's best friend, John "Jay" Novoa, decided to steal it. The problem was that Frank Fappiano, the guy they stole the dope from, was working for a major Mafia boss in the Gambino family.

When I found out that my brother was hanging out with Vinny, I was concerned about it. I knew what type of person Vinny was. I was worried about my brother just associating with him, but my brother never listened. He used to joke around with me. He'd say there was nothing to worry about because Vinny knew us. He always defended him.

About a week before my brother was murdered, I had a dream. We were in a club and Vinny shot my brother in the stomach. He died in my arms. I woke up hysterical. I called my mother—I was living in New Jersey at the time.

"Where's Joey? Where's Joey?"

"I just got off the phone with him. What's wrong?" she asked.

"Oh, my God. I had this really bad dream that something happened to him."

"Call him. I just got off the phone with him."

So I called him.

"Joe, you can't imagine the dream I had. You died in my arms! Vinny killed you. You got shot in the stomach."

He started laughing at me.

"Bubbles, you're so crazy." ("Bubbles" was his

nickname for me. He had nicknames and pet names for everyone.)

"Bubbles, you don't know what you're talking about. Vinny's my friend. He's your friend, too. He always asks about you."

"Joey, he's not your friend. You don't understand. He's the type of guy who will kill you from the back-seat of your own car."

Those were my exact words, but he just blew it off. He didn't listen to me.

When my brother got involved in drugs, he was still protected by my father, so he didn't worry about paying other people if he was dealing in their territory.

These two brothers named Ronnie and Russell Carlucci used to fight with Joey over that all the time. They were fighting over some type of territory. One time my brother set their van on fire. So Joey, Ronnie and Russell were rivals; they didn't like each other from day one. That's why I had such a bad feeling about Joey being involved with Vinny, because Ronnie and Russell were his cousins.

On Friday, March 17, 1995, my mother met Joey at a restaurant in Brooklyn. He told her that one of the guys they robbed the pot from had grabbed him on Eighty-Sixth Street and put a gun to his head. My mother didn't know what he was talking about, so he told her the story.

He told her not to worry because Vinny Rizzuto's father, Vincent "Vinny Oil" Rizzuto, a soldier in the Gambino family, had worked out a deal with Fappi-ano. But my mother knew what that really meant—

Joey was being set up. She told my brother that something was going to happen.

But my brother again said that Vinny's father had straightened everything out.

"I've been in this life for thirty-three years with Daddy. Do not believe them," she told him.

But Joey didn't listen to my mother's warning, either.

That weekend he had decided to go home—his former home, where his wife was living—to spend some time with his daughter, who was four. He wanted to spend St. Joseph's Day, which was that Sunday, March 19, with her. He brought his friend Jay with him. Jay and Joey hung out together all the time. They were so close; they were like brothers.

Joey kept calling me that Sunday. The first time he called, I didn't think anything of it. The second time he called, I asked him what was going on.

"Oh, nothing. I'm just home playing with the baby, watching my wedding video."

He called a few more times and I was getting worried.

"Joe, what's going on? Is everything okay? I never hear from you this many times in a month."

"I was watching my wedding video and you were crying, Bubbles, while I was dancing." Then he kind of laughed. He was making fun of me for crying. Joey had a nervous laugh—like I do. If he was emotional about something, he would laugh about it instead of crying. Although he did cry sometimes, if it was something really serious.

"Why were you crying?"

"What do you mean, why? It was sad—the song and everything, and my little brother getting married."

"You're so stupid, Bubbles."

He called me "Bubbles" because I always laughed. He said I was always bubbly. He very rarely called me Lin. He called my mother "Mrs. Fletcher"—after Jessica Fletcher, the mystery writer and amateur detective—because she always had to know what was going on. He called my father "Papa Smurf."

I thought it was odd that he called me so many times that day. During one of the calls Joey told me that Vinny had been calling him all weekend because he had wanted them to go out on Saturday. My brother, however, wasn't leaving the house. He said he had a funny feeling. He didn't know why, but he just didn't want to go out.

When he told me about it on Sunday, I guess he was a little paranoid because they had ripped off that drug dealer. He knew that something wasn't right, but he didn't really know for sure.

On Monday morning Joey got a call from Vinny, who wanted to meet up. When Joey was leaving the house, his daughter threw a fit-and-a-half. She never wanted him to go, but her mother told us this time was different.

She was hysterical. She was screaming, crying.

"Please, Daddy, don't leave!"

My brother promised her that when he came back, he was going to bring her the biggest doll that Toys "R" Us had. But he never came home.

That day, March 20, 1995, Joey was shot and killed. He was twenty-three years old.

Jay was with him. That's how I know everything that happened in the car. But I didn't get to see Jay right away. I didn't get to talk to him about what happened until much later, because after the shooting he went into protective custody.

When they met up that day, Vinny told Joey and Jay he had a fake credit card and they were going to buy a bunch of stuff with it. Vinny's cousins, Ronnie and Russell, were following in a different car. They couldn't fit into my brother's car.

As they were driving on Brown Street in Sheepshead Bay, Vinny, who was sitting in the backseat, told Joey, "Do me a favor, pull over." My brother pulled over and put the car in park. Right at that moment Jay, who was in the front passenger seat, heard a gunshot. He went deaf because it was so loud. He thought someone was shooting at the three of them in the car. Jay didn't know that it was Vinny.

Jay looked over at Joey and saw a small hole in his head, and the blood was just dripping down. Jay turned around and looked at Vinny, who was holding the gun. He said Vinny didn't even look like Vinny. He looked like the Devil. He looked so evil and vicious. It was as if he had a black soul. Jay told me that in his life he had never seen anybody have the look of the Devil like that.

Then Vinny shot at Jay, who was already halfway out of the car. Jay got shot in the arm. He ran and ran and started screaming and yelling for help. He flagged down a police car and told the cop that his friend was in a car around the block and had just been shot. So there was assistance there pretty quickly. Joey's heart was still beating and he lived until he got to the hospital.

In the meantime Vinny had jumped into the car with Ronnie and Russell. Jay told the police what kind of car they were in. The police chased them, but they got away. Jay became a witness to my brother's murder and went into protective custody.

When my brother was killed, I was living in New Jersey with this guy. We had been living there for about three years. About a week before Joey died, my brother went to see my boyfriend at his work and they got into an argument. When my boyfriend came home that day, he was swearing and yelling, saying he wished my brother were dead.

When the call came that Joey had been murdered, my boyfriend answered the phone. He was in the bedroom and I was in the hallway, but I could hear what he was saying.

"Oh, my God. Where? What happened?"

I started walking toward the bedroom.

"What's going on?"

There was a look of horror on his face. He held the phone out to me.

"My brother?"

I just knew.

"What's wrong? Is it my brother? Is he alive?"

I grabbed the phone. It was Charlie's wife, who was a detective in the Seventy-Eighth Precinct. Charlie remarried after he and my mother divorced.

"They killed your brother."

There was no sympathy in her voice. It was like the world stood still. I started freaking out. Then Charlie got on the phone.

"The bad guys got him. The bad guys got him."

He wasn't making any sense. When I got off the phone, instead of leaning on my boyfriend for support, I started hitting him, kicking him, punching him, punching the walls. The vein in my arm popped out like a bubble, since my fists were going through walls.

"You wished this on him. You wished this on him."

I had to tell my mother. I called for an ambulance to go to my mother's house in Long Island—three hours away. Then I called her. I didn't want her to be told by strangers. When I heard the EMTs knock on her door, I said, "Ma, Joey's with Daddy."

She didn't understand at first.

"What do you mean? Daddy's dead."

Then she started screaming and she collapsed.

The next morning I had to drive to Brooklyn because the family was meeting at my aunt's house. I don't remember why, and I don't even remember how my mother got there because she was in Long Island. It was all such a fog.

On the way I had to drive by Ronnie's and Russell's house and I saw all these cars parked on the block. I hadn't talked to Jay at this point, but I just knew it was Vinny who had killed my brother.

I had experienced hits before, so I knew what happened after a hit. If my father killed someone, his crew came back to the house and all the cars were parked up and down the block.

When I drove by the Carluccis' house, I was scared, but I was also really enraged when I saw all their cars. I just wanted to take a bat and smash every one of them. I didn't do it, but that's how I felt.

When I walked into my aunt's house, I didn't talk to anybody, not even my mother. I can't remember much about. It's buried in my mind somewhere. I know I had to go pick out my brother's coffin with his wife. My uncle came with us and told me it was too expensive and we didn't have the money for it at the time. But I wasn't thinking about that. To be honest, I had no idea who paid for everything.

Joey's wife and my uncle went to identify my brother's body. I asked them how he looked. I wanted to know, but I didn't want to see him. His wife told me he looked peaceful—like he was sleeping. That fact, plus the fact that Jay told me my brother didn't see it coming, made me feel a little better. It didn't comfort me, but at least I knew he didn't suffer.

When I found out that he was killed on Brown Street in Sheepshead Bay, I drove to the exact spot and pulled over to where he was parked. I brought a dozen red roses, which I was going to leave there. I sat in my car for about an hour. I looked around just to see what the last thing was that my brother saw, because Jay said it wasn't Vinny.

While I was parked there, someone came out of one of the houses to ask me who I was and what I was doing. I said that my brother had been killed there, and I just wanted to sit for a while. The person apologized to me for intruding. After that, I tied the roses to a tree and left.

My brother had to be autopsied, so I knew that if there was a wake or funeral, there wasn't going to be an open coffin. I didn't want to see him that way and I know my mother didn't want to, either. None of us wanted to see that. So I pretty much decided that there wasn't going to be anything. Joey wasn't going to be embalmed, because I didn't want anybody else touching him. I remember giving orders about what was going to happen. He was just going to be buried and there would be a priest and a ceremony at the cemetery.

The day that my brother was getting buried, I just couldn't face it. I couldn't face watching my brother go into the dirt with my father underneath him. I couldn't deal with it. It was something that I felt that I would never recover from. I was afraid that I was going to have a nervous breakdown and I wouldn't be able to take care of my son.

My mother collapsed at the cemetery when they were putting him in the ground, and they had to call an ambulance. She was in a psych ward for a month.

So I went to the cemetery when everybody was gone and he was completely covered. I stayed there for the whole day by myself. I was in shock. I couldn't even believe my brother was gone.

I knew then that if I had seen my brother being put into the ground, my life was over. I was never going to recover from that, *never*. And I had a son. I had to be there for my son. My mind was so messed up.

I couldn't deal with the pain of my brother's death. It was an unbearable, unimaginable, inconsolable pain. I couldn't control the pain. It was the most horrible loss that I had ever experienced. I'd be driving and I'd be thinking about my brother and I'd start crying and screaming at the top of my lungs.

"No! Why, God? Why?"

That was in 1995. Today it's not better, not even a little bit.

I don't regret not going to Joey's funeral, because I know that my kids wouldn't have me now. If I had witnessed that, I would not be here today, period.

I wanted to remember my brother the way he was the last time I saw him, which was at my son's birthday party. That day he was having a hard time with his daughter. I yelled at him. I don't remember why. I just got annoyed at him. I felt guilty about that after he was killed.

For a long time nobody ever told my niece that her father had passed away. Everyone kept telling her that he was away, but she was distraught over it. She really loved him. She kept asking for her father. She didn't stop. She kept crying and screaming, "Where's my daddy? Where's my daddy?"

She wasn't getting over it. She remembered the last thing he said to her was that he was going to bring her a big doll from Toys "R" Us.

One day I picked her up to spend some time with her. I couldn't take seeing her pain anymore. It wasn't my place to tell her that her father was gone; it was her mother's place. But her mother couldn't deal with it, either. I knew my brother wouldn't want this for her, so I sat her down and talked to her.

"Honey, I want to talk to you about your dad."

"Okay, where's Daddy? What do you want to tell me?"

I had a giant piece of construction paper and I started drawing a picture of a rainbow, the sky and butterflies. It was a pretty picture.

When I was finished, she asked, "What is that?"

"Do you like it?"

"Yeah, it's really pretty."

"That's heaven."

"Heaven? What's heaven?"

"That's where Daddy is."

"Can I go there?"

"No, honey, not now. You can't go there. But Daddy is there and it's a really nice place. So you don't have to worry about Daddy anymore, because that's where he is."

Of course, she was confused.

"But I want to see him."

"You'll be able to see him, but it's just not going to be now. It's probably going to be a long time from now. But you don't have to worry about him, because he's in a really nice place."

"But I miss him."

"I know you miss him. But keep this picture with you all the time, and every time you miss Daddy, look at the picture and know that that's where he is."

Her mother flipped out on me, but I didn't care. His daughter needed to have some type of closure. And as much as her mother didn't want to admit it, my niece felt better knowing where he was. Not knowing was driving her nuts.

CHAPTER 16

REVENGE

I once dated Joe Rizzuto, the brother of the guy who murdered my brother.

After I broke up with my husband, I decided if I ever dated again, I'd go out with someone who was the complete opposite of him. My ex was a really flashy guy. Always wearing a suit and tie. He was a John Gotti idolizer. I even used to call him that. I wanted to meet a guy who was wearing jeans, sneakers and a white T-shirt.

One night my cousin Charlotte begged me to go out with her because it was her birthday. We went to a club in Brooklyn. We were standing at the bar when my cousin, who knew the type of man I was looking for, said, "Look who just walked in."

"Oh, my God. That guy is gorgeous," I said.

The next thing I knew, he was standing next to me ordering a drink. Of course, I had to flirt. Then we started talking. His name was Joe Rizzuto. My cousin was not too happy—it was her birthday, after all.

"I'm going home because you're ignoring me."

I definitely wasn't leaving, so Joe said he would take me home.

"Charlotte, I'll see you later. I'm going home with him."

"You're not going home with him. You don't even know him."

"No, I mean he's driving me home."

"All right, fine."

When it was time for us to leave, Joe and I walked into the parking lot. I was hoping he would just have a regular car, because I just wanted to be with a regular guy—not someone like my ex-husband who was a show-off. But when he hit the remote control on his keys to unlock the car, I noticed the interior lights of a flashy red Cadillac Allante go on. Even though I thought I wanted a regular guy, Joe was looking pretty good.

When I saw Joe walk in that club that night, it was love at first sight. I was head over heels. When I got home, I ran up the steps into my parents' room to talk to my father.

"Dad, get up."

"What? What's wrong?"

"Dad, I have to tell you something. You don't even know. I just met somebody. Oh, my God. I'm in love."

"What? Go to bed."

"No, Dad. I'm telling you—I'm in love. I swear to God, you have to see him."

"Okay, tell me about it in a little while."

It was so crazy! I had never done that before.

Joe was younger than me. But when we first met, I didn't know exactly how much younger, because he lied to me about his age. I was just about to turn twenty-three and he told me he was twenty. I didn't find out how old he really was until after my brother was killed and the newspapers printed his age. He was five years younger, so that meant he was only eighteen when we started going out.

What's interesting is that he never acted like he was that young. He was very mature. He was driving a nice car and he told me he was working—I found out later that he wasn't. Even if I knew this at the time, it probably wouldn't have mattered.

One day his sister asked me, "How do you feel about going out with such a younger guy?"

I said he wasn't that much younger, but she never told me how old he was.

I used to ask him, "Really, how old are you?"

He'd just laugh and say, "I told you."

He always told me the same age—it was like he was holding on to his lie.

From the night we met, we were inseparable. We were together every single day for a year. He loved me as much as I loved him. That's why it was so hard to get over the fact that he had something to do with my brother's murder.

Joe even had his own apartment. So when my son was with his father for the weekend, I stayed with Joe. We were so connected—we were both crazy for each other.

He became close to my son as well, and he made a bedroom for my son in his apartment. He bought a car bed and made it like a real kid's room. We were always together. We did everything together.

We had a very affectionate relationship. I was so

in love with him. Sometimes when he was sleeping, I would stare at him and touch his face. He was so beautiful and I loved him so much. And he'd do the same. I'd wake up and he would be staring at me. He'd say, "You're so beautiful when you sleep."

That was what hurt me so much. I couldn't believe that I could actually love somebody who could do that to me—a man who could be involved in my brother's murder. That was a very confusing feeling.

My father didn't like Joe much. Maybe it was because Joe's father, Vinny Oil, was tied to the Gambino crime family. There was always some type of awkwardness when they were together—not that we were at my house all that often. It was kind of uncomfortable. It wasn't that my father didn't like Joe; it was more that he wasn't sure about him.

It didn't feel wrong, but it didn't feel right, either. There was just something I couldn't pinpoint. I never really knew the reason, but I didn't care. It wouldn't have mattered what anybody said to me about him.

On one of our first dates Joe brought me to his house to watch the movie *Revenge*. It was about one guy getting revenge on his friend for stealing his wife. That movie gave me nightmares.

Joe and I spent a lot of time at his parents' house. We had dinner there on Sundays. His mother would cook a whole dinner, and we all would be sitting at the table: me, all his brothers and sisters. Then Vinny would start with Joe. They'd go back and forth. Next thing you knew, meatballs were flying. Sauce, spaghetti, meatballs on the ceiling, on the walls, on the table. The table would be flipped upside down. It was because Vinny was so jealous of Joe.

Vinny was a lowlife—not working, sleeping all day. Joe was a lowlife, too. But I didn't see him like that. To me, Joe was a classier kind of guy—always dressed to the nines, clean-cut, with the nicest cars and nicest clothes. Vinny was a street thug, a real dirtbag.

I used to ask myself what I was doing with that family. Joe and I were supposed to get married, but we broke up. Toward the end he wanted to go out without me—to do things with his friends. He started thinking he was a gangster. That's when everything changed and we started to have arguments. Then I caught him with a girl in his car. They weren't doing anything, but he was in the car with a girl. I just ended it after that because I didn't trust him anymore. I didn't want to deal with him.

He came crying to me one day. I told him I wasn't going back with him. To this day I wonder if my brother would still be alive if Joe and I had been married. Would that have saved him and changed everything?

When Vinny killed my brother, it was all about him getting revenge for whatever he thought my brother had done to him. He got revenge on my brother. The revenge I wanted was to see him go to jail.

After my brother was murdered, I called Joe and told him I needed to talk to him.

"You want to talk to me?"

"Yeah, I need to talk to you. We were together for years, and I need to talk to you about some stuff."

"I'm not meeting you." He was afraid to meet me. He thought I was setting him up.

"Meet me in a public place."

"I'll meet you on Eighty-Sixth Street."

"All right, fine. I don't have a problem with that."

When I saw him, I started crying. I was hysterical. Just seeing him, I wanted to kill him. I started punching his chest and he started crying.

"I'm sorry. I'm sorry. I didn't know this was going to happen. I'm so sorry," he repeated.

"How could you let this happen? You knew this was going to happen to my brother, and you should've stopped it. You could've stopped this."

"There was nothing I could do."

That was a load of crap. It came out later that he did know—he planned it.

"There was nothing you could do? Listen, I want to know where your brother is."

"I don't know where he is."

I was sitting with him in his car. I wanted to believe him. I wanted to believe that he didn't know. Joey was my only brother. How could he possibly have known and let it happen? He was supposed to have loved me as much as I loved him.

I had to find Vinny. I was literally putting my life at risk. But I was so messed up. I was a girl who was in the middle of shoot-outs. I lost my father. I lost my brother. My mother was in a psych ward. I was completely on my own. And I was out of my mind.

For a long time I made Joe think I wanted to talk to him and be friends. I was using that as my weapon to get information. I would hang out with him to snoop in his apartment and snoop in his car. I actually gave the detectives two addresses, which I found in his apartment, that were leads to where Vinny was. They followed the leads, but Vinny was already gone.

One day Joe caught me snooping in his bathroom.
"What are you doing, snoopy?"

I laughed, but I was scared.

Well, what are you looking for?"

"I'm not looking for anything. I really should get going."

"Listen, you're not going to find my brother."

"Whatever, I'm not even looking anymore."

That was the last time I saw him. I thought maybe he was going to try to hurt me because he caught me. Joe Rizzuto was a dangerous guy. But at that point I still didn't know that he had conspired to kill my brother. I thought that it was just Vinny and his cousins. I didn't know that Joe was involved.

My mother even went on *America's Most Wanted* to find out where Vinny was. Finally, in June 1998, Joe and Vinny Rizzuto and their cousins Russell and Ronnie Carlucci, described as members of the Gambino and Lucchese crime families, were indicted in the Federal District Court in Brooklyn for Joey's murder, as well as racketeering and drug trafficking. Vinny turned himself in at that time.

Joe took a plea in September 1999 and was sentenced to seventy-eight months in prison—a plea that meant he wouldn't have to admit to planning Joey's murder. He was sentenced only for drug dealing and racketeering. Russell and Ronnie pleaded guilty to racketeering, murder conspiracy for my brother's murder and other charges. Russell was sentenced to 168 months and Ronnie was sentenced to 120 months.

Vinny pleaded guilty to Joey's murder in exchange for a term of eighteen years in prison—but the feds reneged on the deal and the judge gave him twenty-four years. Vinny was sentenced in early 2000. I had so many different feelings, knowing we were going to Vinny's sentencing. I was angry, but I was also afraid to face him. I didn't know what was going to happen, but I knew that my mother and my brother's wife were going to have to stand in front of Vinny and speak. I knew that my brother's daughter—my niece—who was nine years old, was going to have to try to speak in front of the man who killed her daddy.

It was terrifying, because there was so much anger—so much anger to have to face this person and not be able to do anything about it. Just having to sit there and take it and deal with it.

My mother, Joey's wife, his daughter and I went to the courthouse to confront Vinny about murdering Joey and to let him see what he had done to our lives. We had the right to be there. He had his whole entourage of family there. But instead of being sympathetic or showing some remorse or sorrow, they did nothing but spew venom at us. It was pure evil.

His family members were cursing at my mother, cursing at us, blaming everything on us. We were there because Vinny killed my mother's son, my brother, his wife's husband, my niece's father—it wasn't about anything else. But they were making it like we did something to them and it was our fault. It was horrible.

They were like animals in that courtroom. And it was really, really hard to deal with it. My mother was crying, and his family was saying they were "crocodile tears." Joey was her son, and her son was dead. Vinny just stared at us. He kept turning around and giving us this evil, vicious, Devil face. It must have been the same face Jay saw right after Vinny murdered my brother.

I was so scared, not of something happening to me, but just scared of having to see Vinny's face and knowing that it was the face of the person who killed my brother. It was so hideous, so horrifying, to see. Jay said that my brother never turned around and never saw Vinny's face. But just knowing that Vinny's face was the face of evil behind my brother—the face of the person who ended his life—was terrifying.

I was so nervous and very sick to my stomach. I just wanted to throw up. It was very confusing for me because these were people I had been close to at one point. So for me to see Vinny in person for the first time since he killed my brother was extremely confusing. I wanted to know how he could have done it.

I hated him, but, to be honest, part of me felt sorry for him that he could be so evil and do something so bad and ruin everyone's lives. His actions caused nothing but misery and horror for my family. And I'm sure it caused the same thing for his family in a different way. But at least they were still able to see him. We were never going to see my brother again.

The judge let us all speak.

My mother was first. She was crying when she talked to Vinny.

"My son, Joey, stands beside me as he always does. You can't see him now, Vinny, but you saw him the night he was killed and sitting alone in a car to die by himself."

Oh, my God, the daggers Vinny shot with his eyes to my mother. Just like Jay said, he had the look of

evil when he looked at any of us. And his family
acted like we were the criminals. Vinny's mother
yelled at my mother, saying she deserved an Acad-
emy Award because she was such a good actress.

The disrespect and lack of remorse and the dis-
grace that family exhibited in that courtroom was
disgusting.

My mother didn't let them stop her.

"Because of you, Vinny, his life is over. When
Joey was killed, so was my body and mind. My
family's lives have changed so dramatically and we
ask you why you took away a father, a brother, a
husband and my son. He was ripped from my life
and left to die. And I was given no chance to say
good-bye," my mother stated.

Joey's wife, Maria, spoke next. Through her tears
she talked about how Joey loved to spend all the time
he had with their daughter—loving her, playing with
her, teaching her to walk and talk.

She held up a photo of my brother—blown up to
the size of a poster—and told Vinny and the court
about the last day they had with Joey.

"Those were the last kisses, hugs, promises and
smiles she saw. My daughter is always crying and
asking why that bad man killed her daddy. 'Why did
he take my daddy? Everybody at school has their
daddy, but I don't.' I'm here to beg for the maximum
sentencing of Vincent Rizzuto for taking my husband
and a father who can never be replaced to his little
girl," she implored.

Then it was my turn. I was very afraid to go up on
the stand there and talk, and it has been hard for me
to remember if I did or not. My mother said I did

confront Vinny in the courtroom. When I found my victim impact statement recently, I couldn't believe those were the words I spoke, because it was as if I didn't have any emotions. When people are in shock, they're pretty much stone cold.

When I was writing it, I was just putting words on the paper. It wasn't coming from the pain and all the emotions that I really felt. That's because I had, and still have, post-traumatic stress disorder. PTSD is a real thing and I was diagnosed with it. That's why there are certain things I can remember vividly and some things I can't remember at all—and that scares me.

I was diagnosed with PTSD after a couple shootings. My father sent me for therapy because he knew something was wrong. I went to see the therapists, but things didn't always work out. One therapist cried after hearing my story.

"Why are you crying?" I asked him.

"I've never heard a story like this, ever in my life. Your life, your story, it's just so unbelievable."

"Well, I'm not comfortable with you crying."

I thought that was so weird, so I quit that guy. After my father died, and I was living in New Jersey, I found another therapist. He was an older man and I loved him. Talking to him reminded me of talks with my father. I was able to talk to him like he was my father. And since he knew about my father, he wasn't shocked at my story. I felt comfortable talking to that therapist.

One day I was having a meltdown on my birthday, so I called him. He used to tell me his phone lines were always open to me. He said I could call him anytime, day or night.

When I called that day, his daughter answered the phone and told me that her father had passed away that day—on my birthday. I started to cry, begging her to tell me that it wasn't true. I was freaking out that this guy had died. I didn't understand why everybody that I cared about died. He was the best therapist I had ever had, and he died on my birthday. I figured I was not meant to have a normal life. Whose therapist dies on her birthday? That's when I pretty much gave up on therapy.

Even though I don't remember speaking at the hearing, this is what I said to Vinny in that courtroom: "I don't know how to begin to describe the pain and suffering and the heartache that I feel since you took my brother's life—my little brother, Joey. The pain is constant, and the scars are embedded in my mind. I miss my brother, Joey, so much and I can't believe that he's gone. I try to remember the good times and the love that we shared as brother and sister.

"My brother is gone. I don't know why. I thought he would be in this world a lot longer. He had a whole life ahead of him—a life to share with his mother, his sister, his nephew but, most importantly, his daughter that he loved more than life. She was only four when her father was brutally murdered, and this little girl has to live her life without her daddy. You took away her daddy, and the pain this little girl has to deal with will be with her forever.

"Her mother has to watch her daughter, as a single parent, struggle every day with this pain that you caused. I see my mother every day as she struggles to go on, and the pain in her eyes as she tries to get through another day. This is a pain that only a mother feels when she loses a child and I wonder how she will get through this.

"How will his daughter, his mother and myself get through this? I believe the answer to that question is we will have to feel this pain and loss every day and hope we can find a way to cope. We will have to keep my brother's face, his smile, his touch and his laughter strong in our hearts and in our minds. And we will go to sleep at night and pray to God that one day we will be together again."

My niece brought her diary to the hearing. She knew she was going to see the man who killed her daddy. She wanted to read parts of it in court, but she got scared, so the judge read some of it for her.

Then the judge asked Vinny if he wanted to speak. Vinny asked if he could talk without a child in the room. The judge said he couldn't force her to leave. Vinny said he didn't want to say anything bad about my brother in front of his daughter.

My mother and my sister-in-law went nuts. They started screaming at him.

"Did you care about the child when you killed her daddy?"

"Did you care about your victims' families?" Vinny shouted.

At that point his attorney and the court deputy were trying to calm him down.

Vinny pointed to my mother and asked why she was even saying anything to him. Then he went into a rage, screaming about all the people my father killed and the people my brother killed.

While this was happening, my sister-in-law took my niece out of the courtroom. Vinny stopped ranting until she was out the door.

Then he started up again, yelling at the prosecution for going back on the deal they had made with him.

"You think I want to take twenty-four years? I'm never going to see my parents again. My kids are going to be my age when I get out," Vinny told the judge. "What kind of life is that? I wish I would have died. That's it. I wish it would have been me."

In August 2002, Vinny wrote me a letter from prison trying to rationalize why he murdered my brother. He told me he knew it was going to be hard for me to read, but it was also hard for him to write. He said he didn't know how to begin to make me see the truth. He said he was also a victim, but he could never put down on paper what really happened.

He told me when I was dating Joe, he took a strong liking to me and my son. He said he was jealous of his brother because he (Vinny) had a lot of love for me. He said in a world filled with betrayal, envy, hatred and deceit, he hoped that I was focused, maintaining strength of mind and at peace.

As for himself, he said, he was continuously elevated, always mindful that the sun rotates so its rays reach different people and places, causing darkness to descend on others.

He wrote in the letter that he hated what had transpired between us; but when people are surrounded by ignorance on a daily basis, things happen that they sometimes can't get around.

Finally he said he was sorry for my loss and he wished he could see me so he could tell me the truth. He said I would understand then. He said he didn't know what he was doing writing the letter, but he was truly sorry.

But Vinny is wrong. I'll never understand why he killed my brother.

CHAPTER 17

MY MOST
TRUSTED FRIEND

After my father died and my brother was killed, I turned to Tommy McLaughlin, a former member of my father's crew, who was serving fourteen years on a drug charge. It was the worst time in my life, and Tommy reminded me of my father and my brother.

From a very young age Tommy was raised by his sister. His sister had her own life, so he was basically on his own a lot. That's how he got into the street life. He used to come to the house all the time when we were teenagers—we were just about the same age. He liked me and it was obvious. He wasn't like the other guys who were with my father.

For example, sometimes when my father's crew was at the house, I would walk through the living room in a bikini—I had been swimming in the pool—to go up to my room to change. All the other guys looked away, but not Tommy. He looked and he didn't care if my father saw him. My father used to give him a slap on the back of his head.

Tommy had no fear of anything, and he certainly didn't fear my father. That was because he didn't have any bad intentions. And that was the reason he was never afraid to approach me. He always give me a smile or a wink. He had a really strong charm about him. But he also had another side to him—an angry side.

When we got a little older, if he saw me out at a club or somewhere, he got really protective, but not like the other guys in my father's crew who would just tell me to go home. Tommy got angry if he saw me talking to a guy or if I had been drinking.

He had a bite to him—a personality where you didn't know what he was thinking because he could go either way. He could be really sweet and charming, and then he could be really mean and nasty, although never to me. It just bothered him if I was talking to some other guy and I wasn't with him. So when I used to see him in clubs, I tried to avoid him. I was too young for that; I didn't want to deal with it. That's why at first I didn't want to date Tommy. I was having fun and I wanted to keep having fun.

When he found out that I was dating Joe Rizzuto, he was so angry. Every time he saw me, he'd say, "I can't believe you're going out with that loser, white-trash lowlife." He hated Joe. They were rivals. They did not like each other at all. I always thought Tommy hated Joe more than Joe hated Tommy.

After Joe and I broke up, I had started hanging out more with Tommy. One day Joe came to my house, crying and apologizing to me. But I didn't want anything to do with him after he cheated on me. I was trying to move on. I already had talked to Tommy and I wanted to go out with him. So Joe left.

When we were together, Tommy was very affectionate and sincere. I felt comfortable with him. And he was always on my side—it didn't matter what I said or did, I was always right.

During the Colombo war Tommy was dealing drugs, and the Brooklyn DA was out to get him. They thought he could lead them to his bosses. Two Brooklyn cops were getting ready to arrest him in September 1992, but the war got worse and Tommy went into hiding.

A couple months later, Tommy invited me to go to the wedding of a Colombo family member in Brooklyn. It was going to be our first official date. On the day of the wedding Tommy looked so nice—he always looked nice—and he smelled really good, too.

While we were at the reception, which was at the Embassy Suites hotel, he told me he spotted some cops there and he was going to get arrested. He said he needed me to help him get out of there. I didn't know what the hell was going on.

So Tommy told me what to do, and that's what I did. Tommy went into a bathroom and climbed out the window; I was standing outside another bathroom. So when the cops came and asked me where he was, I pointed into that bathroom. But he was never in there. He was already out the window and gone. I didn't see him again until after he was in jail.

The cops finally caught up to him in December. He called to tell me he had been arrested. By then, I knew I wanted to be with him. I didn't know the extent of his trouble, but I wanted to be with him regardless.

I found out later he had been arrested on charges of racketeering, extortion, firearms, drug trafficking, and tax evasion. They offered to cut him a break if he testified against the other guys, but he refused. Tommy pleaded guilty to one charge of selling cocaine and one charge of tax evasion. He got fourteen years in state prison for selling coke and nine years— to run at the same time as the state charges—for the tax evasion.

At first, he was in the Brooklyn House of Corrections and I went to visit him as much as I could. The visits were rough at the Brooklyn House. There was no contact and you had to sit on the opposite sides of the table. But I still went to try to make him feel better and lift his spirits.

There was one day when he called to tell me he couldn't have a visit. I was already getting ready to leave my house and I had it in my head that I was going to see him, not matter what. I remembered that he could see me from a particular window. I told him to look out that window at three o'clock in the afternoon and I would be outside.

"Don't come all the way here for that," he said.

"I have something to show you, so go by the window. I'm coming to see you. I don't care if it's through the window."

He finally agreed. So I went and got this big poster board and wrote with a black marker in big, thick letters so he could see it: TOMMY, I LOVE YOU. He came by the window at that time and I held up the poster.

He had a big smile on his face. He called me later and said, "I can't believe you came all the way here and did that. You made my day. I was so happy." At that point we were getting really close.

After one visit I left Tommy and went to see my father, who was in the hospice with the marshals at that time. When I got to the room, I ran, crying, into my father's arms. I said that I loved Tommy and I wanted to be with him. I wanted to know what I was going to do. It was so emotional, even the marshals were becoming emotional. They were looking at me crying on my father's shoulder. I could tell they felt bad.

"I want to marry him. I want to be with him," I told my father.

"Do whatever makes you happy. You have my blessing to marry him if you want to marry him," he said. "But you have to tell him he has to take off the 'Mc' from his name." He was joking to make me laugh. Even the marshals laughed.

When Tommy was in the Brooklyn House, I would see him as much as I could. When my son was with his father on weekends, I would go. Whenever I could see him, I would.

But then they transferred him from the Brooklyn House, I think it was to Rikers Island and the visits became harder and less frequent. It was harder for us to talk, and we just grew apart—not by choice but because of circumstance.

Then my father died in June 1994; and in March, the next year, my brother was murdered. I really didn't see Tommy during that time. About six months after my brother was killed, I went to Tommy's sister's house. She was so angry at me. She was yelling and screaming.

"Where have you been? We needed you and you were nowhere to be found!"

"I just lost my family. What are you talking about? I don't even know what you're saying. My brother died. I don't understand what you're saying."

I didn't have any idea what was going on. I hadn't been following what was happening with Tommy because I had so much stuff happening to me.

"We needed you in court," she said.

She said he had had other charges brought against him.

"Where is he? I want to see him."

So I went to see him. At that point he was in Green Haven Correctional Facility in upstate New York. He was kind of standoffish and had his guard up a little bit. I cried and told him that I was sorry and missed him. He hugged me because of my brother. He couldn't believe it. He tried to comfort me but he really didn't know how to react to me.

Then I asked him a question that kind of shocked him.

"Do you want to get married?"

"You're asking me?"

"Yeah, I want to be with you. I've realized a lot of things."

"Do you understand how much time I have?"

I told him that I didn't care. I said that I loved him, and I wanted to be with him. So we planned to get married, but it was going to be a secret. I was afraid of my son's father finding out, then taking me to court for marrying someone who was in prison for drugs. So I kept it a secret from everyone—not even my mother knew. At first, nobody knew I married Tommy except for his family.

While he was in Green Haven, I visited him all the time—it was part of my life. If my son was with his father, I was at the prison. Once we got married, we were able to have overnight weekend visits. I only got to have one weekend visit with him, which I completely ruined.

Back then I was suffering from massive anxiety and panic attacks. So when I went up for that visit to be with him for the weekend, I nearly had a heart attack. We were in a room that was locked from the outside and I couldn't get out when I wanted. We could go outside, but the guards had to let us out.

I was freaking out being locked up. If I looked out the window, all I could see was a huge wall surrounding the prison and the guards. Tommy tried to calm me down.

"Let's go outside and get some air."

"No, I can't. You don't understand. I have to leave. I have to get out of here."

There was a phone in the room for visitors to use if they wanted to leave. But if you picked up that phone, your visit was over. That was it. I wanted to call to get out.

"Linda, please."

"I have to get out of here."

"Just calm down. I'm here with you."

"I can't calm down. I can't. You don't understand. I can't calm down. I have to go."

I ended up staying, but it was not a good weekend. I wasn't able to calm down. I was freaking out the whole weekend. Even though it was just a different atmosphere, which we needed so we could be alone and spend time together, I knew I could never do it again.

He wanted me to come again on a weekend visit. We were planning it, but I kept making excuses why I couldn't make it. I was so afraid to go up there. I wanted to spend time with him, but it was too scary for me. I didn't like the feeling at all.

Before that weekend, though, we had had so many talks about us having a life together, and having kids. I used to tell him that we were going to have twins—it's ironic that I did end up having twins, but with someone else—and I was going to name them Tammy and Tommy. He used to laugh and tell me I was crazy. I was convinced that I was going to have these twins with him.

When Tommy was first sent to Green Haven, he was trying hard to be there for me. He called me as much as he could. One time I was sick and I couldn't get to the store to get the things I needed. The next thing I knew, one of his friends was at the door with milk and groceries. I couldn't believe that he was able to accomplish that while he was so far away from me. He took better care of me while he was in prison than some people took care of me on the outside.

While he was away, Tommy promised that he was going to stay out of trouble, but it was really hard for him. He had a very strong and aggressive personality when he was put in certain positions. Being in jail, you're put in those positions all the time. I was twenty-something years old and didn't understand that. I told him to stay out of trouble and go to school.

He told me he was going to get his GED, and do this and do that; he wouldn't get in any trouble. When Tommy got in trouble, we couldn't speak for days or weeks. It would make me so angry that I couldn't talk to him. The prison would take his phone privileges away.

I tried to spend time with his family to fill the void. To me, being close to his family was like being close with him. He liked when I was around his family, too. I really didn't have anybody. I had just lost my father and my brother, and I didn't have my niece. My mother was living in Long Island at the time, so I was trying to make his family my family. I wanted to be close to them.

The reason I turned to Tommy after I lost my brother was because a lot of people turned their backs on us. I felt that no matter what happened between Tommy and me, I could always go back to him and he would be there for me. Before anything else he was my friend.

I was right. Even though Tommy was hurt because we had lost contact for a while, he didn't turn me away when I went to see him after Joey was killed. The reason I called him "my most trusted friend" was because that's exactly what he was. I could turn to him, no matter what.

Tommy also experienced a loss while he was in prison. His mother died while he was away. I was the person who had to tell him. When he called, I told him I had to speak to him and it was very important. I told him to call me when he was alone.

"I don't want you around anybody," I said.

"What's going on?"

"I need to tell you something very important, but I need you to be alone—as best as you can be alone."

"Okay, I'm going to call you back."

He did a short while later.

"What's wrong?"

"Tommy, I'm really sorry, but your mother passed away."

He was in shock.

"Are you fucking kidding me? I can't believe I'm in here."

Even though his sister raised him, he loved his mother. He was so upset. I tried to comfort him the best I could over the phone. It was a difficult time that we had to get through. At least he was able to go to his mother's funeral.

As time went on, Tommy wasn't staying out of trouble. He wasn't doing what he said he was going to do: go to school and get his GED. I wasn't happy about that, and our relationship started to suffer. Then something happened that totally destroyed our marriage.

I had a lot of expensive jewelry at my house, but I didn't think it was safe there. I asked Tommy's sister to keep it for me for a little while because she had an alarm system. There was a lot of jewelry and I trusted her with it. Why wouldn't I? I was married to her brother.

When things started going bad between Tommy and me, I called his sister and asked her for my jewelry. She told me she had already given it back to me.

We got into a huge fight because she was lying to me. She had never given anything back to me.

But there was nothing I could do. I went to the cops, but they told me I didn't have any proof. Then I told Tommy the whole story. I was shocked at how he reacted.

"She would never do that."

"Tommy, don't tell me she wouldn't do that—she did it. Please, just tell her to give me my stuff," I told him, although I wasn't quite sure what she had done with it.

That caused such a problem for him and me. After all, she was the person who was taking care of him while he was in jail. She was the one who sent him money. She was the one who sent him clothes. She was the one who sent him food. I didn't have any money to send him anything. He couldn't fight with her or he'd have nothing.

Tommy was put in a bad position. I was his wife, and she was his sister who raised him and was still taking care of him. He didn't know what to do. He was in jail, so there really wasn't much he could do. I was yelling and screaming at him that his sister stole from me. He just kept saying she wouldn't do that to me.

Finally I decided I couldn't be part of that family any longer. I could never forgive my sister-in-law for what she did. Tommy and I just faded. We broke up. It was just over and I filed for divorce.

I really loved Tommy. He always reminded me so much of my father and brother. It was his personality, his strength. He was a protector. He knew how to love me. He was the only man who truly loved me. And that's what makes it so sad.

All these years I went from one bad relationship to another, even though I had someone who really loved me, and I really loved him. I should have waited for him. It would have been hard, but I could have done it. By the time he got out, I was basically still on my own. But there was no going back—he had met someone else, gotten married and had a kid.

Shortly after Tommy got out of prison in 2008, he flipped. He was arrested for a murder he had committed with his uncle, Thomas Gioeli, seventeen years earlier. He didn't want to go back to prison. He became an informant for the federal government and basically "brought down the Mob."

I didn't even know that he had turned at first. I did know that he never wanted to go back to prison. Before he went to jail on the drug charges, he told me he had something big hanging over his head. However, he never told me what that was. At that time I told him he should flip and go into witness protection. I wanted to go with him and then we could have had a life away from everything.

Before he went to jail, he told me he would never rat. I told him whatever it was that he did was going to come back to haunt him. I said the feds were going to wait until he did his fourteen years on the drug charges. Then, when he was ready to walk out that door, they were going to nail him. But he didn't want to hear it. Well, guess what? That's exactly what they did. Tommy really didn't have any choice but to flip. After doing fourteen years, I'd flip, too.

When I found out that Tommy got out of jail, I wanted to see him. I didn't know he had a girlfriend. I didn't know he was an informant for the feds. I didn't know much of anything about him, but I wanted to see him. I thought that he would contact me, but he didn't. (It was probably because he was under surveillance—he hadn't testified for the feds yet—and also because he had a girlfriend.)

Because I didn't know any of that, I used to drive by his sister's house, hoping I would see him. I hated his sister, so I couldn't just go to the front door and ring the bell. Still, I wanted to see him.

One day when I drove by, he was outside getting an ice cream from the ice-cream truck. I pulled up and called out, "Tommy." His hair wasn't brown anymore; it was completely gray. When he saw me, he turned white. I knew he was nervous. It was pretty awkward. I asked him how he was and I told him I had been dying to see him. He wasn't himself, though.

Then a woman started screaming out of the window, asking him who I was.

"Is that your girlfriend?" I asked.

He just smirked.

"Okay, I just wanted to see you."

"It was nice to see you," he said.

"You too."

Later I reached out to him on Facebook. I said I was happy to see that he was happy because he deserved it. He never responded.

CHAPTER 18

NOBODY WON
THIS THING

Lin DeVecchio was one of the few FBI agents ever charged with murder. His crime: leaking information to my father about the whereabouts of mobsters from a rival Colombo faction—mobsters my father was trying to kill. The case was dismissed when Lin's attorney discredited a key witness—my mother—during the trial. But she was telling the truth about how Lin helped my father. I know because I was there.

On March 30, 2006, Lin was indicted for taking bribes from my father in exchange for giving him information that helped him murder Joseph "Joe Brewster" DeDomenico, Lorenzo "Larry" Lampasi and Nicholas "Nicky Black" Grancio—as well as Mary Bari. Lin pleaded not guilty.

On November 1, 2007—in the middle of the trial—the lead prosecutor, Mike Vecchione, dropped the charges because he said his star witness against Lin—my mother—didn't tell the truth in court.

During the trial reporters Tom Robbins and Jerry Capeci came forward with tapes of interviews that they had done with my mother years earlier. They were planning to write a book with her, and they indicated that she told them different accounts of certain events than she was giving at Lin's trial.

I maintain she was telling the truth at Lin's trial, and everybody knew she was telling the truth. The prosecutors all knew about those tapes because my mother told them. My mother can explain everything that happened

I told them I was heavily medicated and I was still protecting Lin at that time. I told them that these tapes I did were out there. I said, "I did numerous interviews with different writers to do a book, and I told different stories." But they said they didn't care. When the FBI guys came to my house to ask me about Lin, I lied to them, too, saying Lin didn't help Greg.

Then a friend of mine from the FBI, a really nice guy, called me and told me the other FBI agents knew I was lying. He told me the other agents were going to come back to talk to me and I should just tell them the truth. But, of course, I didn't tell them the whole truth about the murders. I told them that Greg gave Lin jewelry, including an antique ring for his mother, and he gave him jewelry for his girlfriend and his daughter.

I remember the time that Lin was going crazy to

get his daughter a Cabbage Patch doll. So Greg had his gangster friends get the doll for Lin. I used to cook for Lin all the time, eggplant parmigiana. Even when the war was going on, he would come to the house and go through the back entrance. When Greg had to call Lin, I would back the car up to the back door, so Greg could get in the backseat and then get down on the floor. I would drive Greg to the phone—guys, meanwhile, are looking to kill him—and he'd call Lin.

When the DA's office sent people to my house to convince my mother to testify against Lin, they told her they had other witnesses who were going to confirm her story. They said they had a rock-solid case against Lin. I wasn't buying it.

"You're not going to beat the FBI," I told them.

"How can you say that we're not going to win?"

"Well, first of all, the FBI isn't going to let Lin go down and then have to let twenty-five or thirty or maybe more Mafia guys get retrials and let them all get out of jail."

I believed that's just what happened.

During her testimony my mother told the court about the money my father paid Lin for the information that he used to murder people. She even explained that before Lin came over to the house, she'd pull the blinds and lock the doors. All through her testimony my mother told the court what she was saying was fact.

I was supposed to testify as well. I had been scheduled for the day after the charges against Lin were ultimately dropped. I was going to tell the truth about what I saw—when Lin was at the house, I saw my father give him envelopes with money in them. And my father did cover the doors when he came over. Lin even went on vacation with us to our house in Florida. What FBI agent does that?

Lin also called the house a lot and I'd answer the phone. Whenever he had to talk about something that he didn't want my father to talk about on the house phone, he would make my father call him from another phone, either a pay phone or the phone downstairs in my aunt's apartment.

When my brother and I were younger, my parents would take us when they had to leave the house if my father had to call Lin from the pay phone. We'd sit in the backseat and wait for him to get off the phone. Lin had a phone called the "hello" phone, which my father used to call when he wanted to reach Lin.

The DA knew about the tapes because Tom Robbins, one of the reporters, wrote about them during the trial. He was summoned to appear before the judge on October 31, about a week after his story was published. At that meeting the prosecutor said he was going to drop the case if the tapes confirmed what was in Robbins's story.

So, on November 1, the DA's office knew they were going to flip the case on my mother, but they didn't tell us. Then before she was to get back on the stand that day, someone talked to her and confused her. The result was that she said the opposite of what she had been saying all along.

Of course, when she said that at trial, all hell broke loose. The judge told her she could face perjury charges. After that happened, I called the cop who had initially approached my mother about testifying against Lin. I was flipping out about what they were doing to my mother.`

"Don't worry. Your mother is going to be found not guilty of perjury. Don't worry."

It was like he knew already.

"How do you know?"

"Don't worry. It will work out."

He was right. A special prosecutor decided there wasn't enough evidence to charge my mother with perjury either for what she said before the grand jury or at trial.

CHAPTER 19

A DAY IN THE LIFE

I love my father, and I always will, but I have anger and resentment toward "the life." It's a life of horror—filled with nothing but misery, death and nightmares. This life destroys everything around you.

When you marry someone in the Mob or are conceived by someone in the Mob, there is really no way out of it. You lose people you love. There is so much pain you can't get over it. I live with the pain every day, as do the families of my father's victims. But I don't expect tears, nor do I want sympathy.

When I was a child, the man I knew was very loving, affectionate, caring and protective. As I got older, I knew what he was. I knew that he was in the Mafia, and I knew what he did. But I still loved him. I didn't agree with the things that he did, but he was always there for me when I needed him.

He was like Jekyll and Hyde. One minute, in the house, he would be this big teddy bear who would sit there and watch *Wheel of Fortune* with us—we'd all guess the letters—and *Family Feud*. I mean he would play video games with us, laugh and joke around. He'd bake and cook. He was so sensitive when it came to us.

Once he left the house, he was a different person. In some circumstances he was still a very caring person. When he was sick, I used to go to Manhattan with him when he had to get transfusions. He'd give out money to homeless people there. He would pull over if he saw somebody in the streets cold or hungry, and he would give them $100. So he did have this other, caring side to him.

But when he left the house to be the person that he was in the streets, he was completely different. He could walk out of the house and go shoot someone. I could hardly believe some of the stories I heard. I told myself he couldn't have done those things. But he did.

Although he was a killer before the war, he was a true-blue father. He was a loving, caring, protective— maybe to an extreme—father. In his book, the son of an infamous Mafia crime boss said his father chose the life before he chose his family. That's not the case with us. In the beginning my father chose us before he chose the life, until he knew he was going to die of AIDS.

But then he had to show the world that he was still strong, even though the disease was going to ravage his body. He wanted people to know that even though he had a disease that was going to kill him, he was still who he was. He was still powerful and he was still going to fight the fight. I don't think he really wanted to wage the war. I think he wanted to prove to people that he still was strong. But once they tried to kill him in front of us, then he lost it.

My father wasn't the monster people make him out to be; he was a gangster. But his fatherly instincts always took over. AIDS, revenge and anger were fueling my father, and he was in a position where he didn't care about his life anymore. He knew his life was going to end, and he wanted to be sure he got those people back for what they did to his family. He was thinking about us, but in way that wasn't rational because he had lost control because of AIDS.

It still boggles my mind, though. I can't figure out to this day how he was able to be two different people—if not more. I haven't been able to make sense of any of it. I'm still tormented by it, because there's the person I love and want to remember. Then I hear all these things, and sometimes I get angry. But then I go to the cemetery, and I'm not angry anymore. It's just constant turmoil that I have to deal with.

And I think about the other families that he destroyed, and that hurts. I know what that feels like because of what happened with my brother. When I think about the other people that he did that to, it's very painful and disturbing.

My brother and I—and I'm sure other kids in the life feel this way, too—we had this curse that never goes away. You have to deal with the pain for the rest of your life, especially if you lost a sibling or parent. It doesn't ever go away—it stays with you forever. Holidays and birthdays are not the same, but my brother's murder was the worst pain that I have ever felt.

Not too long ago a mutual friend introduced me to Wild Bill Cutolo's son. Wild Bill's son was dealing with the same kind of pain because we're both children of people who were in the Mob.

We've been talking on the phone, trying to make sense of a life where no one thought twice about killing a friend or a former friend. We want to continue our new friendship in the hopes that it will help us get past the sins of our fathers that haunt us to this day.

Recently I also spoke to Vic Orena's son. The first time we talked, it was very strange. It was something that was hard to imagine—two kids brought into the same type of family, whose fathers were rivals and out to get each other. Now we're friends, and that's also kind of strange.

He let his dad know that we were speaking, and he said his father was very happy that we were talking. Before the war started, my father and Vic were acquaintances. They weren't really friends. I don't even know if they really liked each other, but they had to get along.

But once the war started, that was it. They became enemies. My father wanted him badly, and he was doing everything in his power to try to find him. And Vic was after my father. It was kill or be killed, whoever found the other one first.

But neither of them found the other; they were both pretty smart, calculating men who knew how to protect themselves. That's why they both stayed alive.

The reality of living this life is . . . I'm not sure

how to explain it. If I met someone now, and he was fascinated by someone in the Mafia, or she was bragging about dating somebody in the Mafia, I would tell this person that the life has nothing but horror, misery, nightmares and death. Not that anyone would listen. I'm sure this individual wouldn't listen. Everything horrible in life that you could ever imagine *is* really in that life. Nothing good ever comes out of being in that life.

All the money that you have at that time, it doesn't matter. There is no amount of money that could bring back someone that you love. And once you're in that life, and you lose someone, that's the only way you're going to know what I'm talking about.

One of my biggest fears in my life, even when I was younger, was that I was going to go crazy. I could never watch movies like *Girl, Interrupted* or any movies where there was somebody who was crazy and got locked up.

That's probably why I was so scared to go to the weekend visits with Tommy, because I didn't like being locked up. And I was afraid I would go crazy because of everything I had gone through in my life.

I was always trying to be strong and keep it together. I wanted to be there for everybody else, and I was really never there for myself. When the war happened, and my father got sick and died and my brother was murdered, I thought there was no way that I could experience those things without going crazy.

I finally got over that fear. I figured, I was already crazy, but I've been out in the real world and haven't been locked up. Recently I went to a new therapist, but I was afraid to tell him everything because I didn't want him to think that I was sick and needed to be locked up.

I've kept it together for my kids. My kids have always been the reason why I stayed strong, when I really wanted to fall apart.

There have been days when I couldn't get out of bed. I literally spent a month in bed one summer when my son was with his father. I got up just to have something to eat and drink, and then I went back to bed. I was sleeping twenty hours a day for that whole month. When I knew that my son was coming back home, I had to pull myself together.

Every March 20—the anniversary of my brother's murder—I watch my mother suffer through the day. It's a sad life. It's been over twenty years since he was killed but it never gets any better. My kids make me happy, of course, but there's always that void.

I've missed out on so much, not having my brother there for so many life events. Not being able to call him on the phone. Not being able to hear his laugh. Not being able to hear him joke about the stupidest things, and make up the craziest nicknames for everybody. Joey had a free spirit. He tried not to let things bother him, but he got mixed up in the wrong life.

After he died, I felt so alone. I ended up in a violent relationship, where I was abused, and I didn't have anyone to turn to. I was afraid, and nobody was there for me.

One thing about being in this life is that when the shit hits the fan, everybody runs. And the people who run, they don't come back. The people you care for are dead, and you don't even know where you are half the time.

My nephew Gregory Scarpa III, Greg Junior's son, grew up in the life, too. It wasn't easy for him, either. He was eight or nine when his father went to prison in 1988. I've asked my nephew to share his story.

The first thing I'd like to say is that the man everybody called "the Grim Reaper" was "Grandpa" to me. He was always a very good, kind, loving grandfather. I heard the stories when the Colombo war broke out, and I was exposed to some things, but he was still my grandpa. It was just a bad situation.

After my father went away, things got really hard for my mother and me. She had to work a lot so she left me with family. We were living in Staten Island. There were a few relatives I could have spent time with, but I wanted to go to my grandfather's house because I loved my grandfather and my uncle Joey. Joey was like my older brother and I followed him around everywhere.

When I was young, my grandfather would sometimes take me with him to his meetings. I was about six years old, and he was probably fifty-eight or so, although I didn't know that then. To me, he was an old man. He was my old grandpa. He wanted to be sure no one was following him, so we hopped fences in Brooklyn, going from one neighborhood to another. Then we took one car to another car to another and eventually we arrived at the meeting place.

Of course, that doesn't sound normal now, but I was a little boy then and it was great. I used to hop fences in Staten Island with my friends, and then I was doing it with my grandfather. I thought that was cool.

Before the war I used to spend overnights at my grandfather's house. AIDS had started to set in, but I didn't really understand at that age. I figured Grandpa was a little sick, but he still had a lot of love for me and he loved my mom, Lillian. My dad was married three times, and my grandfather always said my mom was his favorite.

I used to go to his Wimpy Boys Social Club with my father and I'd hang out there pretty much all day. There was this one guy, Anthony Scarpati, or Scappy, who used to tease me all the time. Aunt Linda said he used to tease my uncle Joey all the time, too. Scappy was my godfather. All the guys would tease me, but Scappy would actually hurt me. He gave me noogies and put bumps on my head.

Scappy was the boss, which is probably why my father never protected me from him. I didn't know who to hide behind. But if my grandfather was there, I knew I had someone to hide behind. If Scappy was teasing me and I ran to my grandfather, Scappy would stop dead in his tracks and I knew I was safe. I always felt so safe around my grandfather.

I didn't know the seriousness of his illness until I heard that he was going to be on television. I found out that he had AIDS when I saw him on the news. I watched him admit to the world that he had AIDS. But I couldn't understand why my grandfather had to go on television and admit to the rest of the country that he had this virus. Why my grandfather?

That's when I understood that he was a pretty important guy and I started putting everything together—like what my dad was doing and how important and powerful my grandfather was.

I'll never know for sure if my dad knew what my grandfather was doing with the FBI, because nobody ever talked to me about it at the time. Like I said, he was Grandpa, and my dad was my dad. It was a normal family to me.

Life started to get hard for me because of what was going on. I clung to my grandfather because my dad was taken away from me when I was so young. Then when I realized I was going to lose my grandfather, either to jail or to an illness, it made it even harder for me. I started to act out as a kid. Then it got worse after I lost my grandfather; and shortly after that, I lost my uncle Joey, and I worshiped him.

That wasn't the way it was supposed to be.

When my dad went away, my mom used to take me to my grandfather's house in Brooklyn for dinner or maybe because she had to talk to him about something.

I remember like it was yesterday, when my grandfather told me, "When your father is about to be released, me and you are gonna take a helicopter to the prison, and we're going pick your father up in a helicopter."

And I believed my grandfather 100 percent. I started living my life believing that when I turned twenty-one, my father was going to be released. That made things a little easier for me, having that in the back of my mind. That's what kept me from really losing it at a young age. I knew I couldn't lose it completely, because my father was going to be coming home.

I also believed my grandfather was going to live through this illness. He wasn't going to go to jail and he wasn't going to lose his life in some war on the street in Brooklyn. I believed that we were going to pick up my father someday in a helicopter from the prison in Lewisburg, Pennsylvania, where he was at the time, and we were going to live happily ever after.

It didn't work out that way. I'm thirty-five now and I was diagnosed with multiple sclerosis when I was twenty-nine. At that time I was actually working for a local laborers union, Local 731, which is outdoor laborers. I had been working for them for two years, and they had me on high-profile jobs. I worked on the new Yankee Stadium for nine months. The first day I walked onto the Yankee Stadium site, it was pretty much all dirt—they were pouring the concrete. By the time I left there, the grass was down and the dugouts were in. It was beautiful. I'm a huge Yankee fan, so that was a big thing.

When my grandfather was around, I never feared anything. If I was ever afraid and he was around, I ran to him before my own father. I was very close to him and I still am. I feel a major connection to him. I've always felt that he's my higher power—and I feel that way today.

CHAPTER 20

ONE MORE SECOND WITH MY BROTHER

After my brother died, I used to drive by his house in Staten Island all the time when it was empty and just stare at the house. Then finally I had the courage to go in. I used to open the door and call out his name—that's what I used to do when he lived here. I'd call out "Joe," just to let him know I was there. I did that for a long time because it made me feel like he was there. Finally I decided that I wanted to live in that house. I bought it and lived there from about 1996 to 2005.

It's so hard for me to remember some things about my brother. But I want to tell you what I do remember. Even though we were only two years apart, we were worlds apart. We had different friends and we were completely different. We really didn't hang out. When we lived on Avenue J, we used to play outside together and play video games with my father. We did a lot of things together, but we still fought like crazy. We'd always get in trouble for that, because my mother and father hated it when we were fighting.

We were a real family on Avenue J, having dinner together every night. We loved that house. But once we moved to Eighty-Second Street, everything changed. It destroyed our lives in a lot of ways. There were no more rules. Joey wanted to go out; I was going to clubs. There was no more family. Maybe that's why I have such a hard time remembering.

One of the things I do remember is when Joey met his wife, Maria. She was dating one of his acquaintances. My brother was head over heels for her. He fell totally in love with her. He loved everything about her. She was all he talked about. He had to have her.

At the time there was a song out called "Maria" by TKA. Joey played that song for her over and over. Actually, I still can't listen to that song or I'll fall apart. If you listen to the words, they pretty much described his life when he met her. The Maria in the song was dating another guy, and there was this other guy who was crazy about her. He was trying to get her away from him. When Joey met his Maria, she was with another guy, and Joey was trying to get her away from him. The words just tell the story about how Joey felt about Maria and what he was going through.

Maria finally broke up with that other guy. When she did, she and Joey started dating. They dated for a year or so; then they decided to get married. They had their wedding at the La Mer reception venue. My brother was hysterical at his wedding. Somebody had given him gum before he got there, so he was chewing gum during the ceremony.

The priest was talking about love and he kept saying the word "love" again and again. Finally my brother said, "Okay, I get it. *Love.*" He was just so funny.

The wedding and the reception were beautiful, but Maria's father wasn't quite sure how everything was going to turn out. He wore a bulletproof vest to his daughter's wedding because he thought he was going to get shot.

My father was sitting at one of the tables talking with him when he realized the guy was wearing the vest.

"Are you wearing a vest? Is that a bulletproof vest?"

My father nearly wet himself; he was laughing so hard. He could not believe this guy wore a bullet-proof vest to his daughter's wedding. This was a joke for the longest time.

I was never sure how Maria's family felt about my father, since they never let the real truth out. If they didn't like him, they weren't going to show it. But when my father was sick, Maria's mother used to make him a lot of food every day. He'd tell her, "I don't have a stomach. Where do you want me to fit all this?" She would tell him to "eata the food." I guess they did like one another, because why else would she do that?

When they first got married, Joey and Maria lived in an apartment, but I don't remember where it was. It wasn't long before they started looking at houses and they bought a fully furnished town house in

Staten Island. All they took with them was their clothes. It was a beautiful house—it was the model home. Then they had a baby and there they were, two kids living in this house with a baby.

Joey wasn't working—he was dealing drugs in the streets. He wanted to open up a business, but he didn't know what to do or how to go about it. He just knew he didn't want to continue to do what he was doing.

He tried to talk to my father about how to start a business and what to do, but he just couldn't get it done. When you get caught up in making fast money, it's really hard to get out of it—it's really hard to get away from it.

My brother really was a good person—he wasn't a bad guy. He didn't want to hurt people. He didn't act like a tough guy. Sure, he had problems in the street and he did act that way, but that was over territory and stepping on each other's toes in the neighborhood.

He never used all his training in karate on anybody, either. He wasn't that type of person. He had been taught by the karate teacher never to use his training in the street unless it was self-defense. He lived by that.

I've always felt that our lives were kind of rushed. We both got married so young. But I believe it was supposed to be that way because his life ended so fast. At least he got to do things that most kids his age wouldn't have been able to do. It wasn't the norm to get married at nineteen and have a baby.

We actually had our kids around the same time. My son was born in March 1990, and his daughter was born in November of that year. They used to play together.

But after Joey and Maria had the baby, things started to change. Her mother started becoming overly protective. She didn't want Maria and the baby to come to our house or spend time with us on holidays. I wasn't sure why she felt that way. Maybe she was being protective, because she thought that some bad things were going on.

My brother was upset about it. He wanted his daughter to be part of our family, just like I wanted my son to be around my parents. We were both dealing with the same problems—in-laws who wanted us to be with them and not with our own family.

We knew that my father wasn't well and we were trying to do everything we could for him. It seemed like it was harder for us to leave our parents. Maybe it was because we were so young, but my brother and I wanted to be home with our family, and we wanted our kids there. I guess it was hard for our in-laws, too.

After we both separated from our spouses, there was a time when Joey and I were living back home and the kids were with us. We let the kids run wild in my parents' house. They pretty much wrecked it. My father was always saying, "Somebody watch these kids over here—they're wrecking my TV!" Or he'd say, "Can someone stop the baby? She's eating a cigarette." It was pretty funny. Then after my father died, our relationship with Joey's daughter was pretty much over.

Most of our lives there was always something that kept Joey and me from spending time together. Once we were living back home, we were able to see each other, one-on-one, and we had some good times.

One night we went to a club together in Long Island. It was strange to see my brother in a club; I never had when we were teenagers. He was a lot of fun. He had a couple drinks and he was laughing most of the night. I was really surprised.

As I look back to when I lost my brother, I realize I've missed out on so much with him. It bothers me a lot. I never got to have that relationship that a brother and sister have when they get older.

In my heart I've always believed that we would have been the best of friends and we would have been there for each other. I knew we were going to become really close. I'm not just saying that because he's gone. I'm saying it because of how I felt before he died.

It makes me sad that we didn't have a chance to become close. All of a sudden he was gone. That was something that I was never able to come to grips with and it bothers me to this day. I carry a lot of guilt over it and I think that's part of the reason why I block out so much of my time with my brother.

I live with this guilt because I feel that I could've done or said so much more to him in the time that I had. I often hear people say, "My grandmother lived until she was ninety. She had a long and happy life, and we had so much time to spend together."

Well, I didn't have that time. My brother was taken when he was twenty-three. But then there are people who say, "Well, I had five years with my child, and at least I had those five years." I had more time than those parents, but I still didn't have the time that I should have had with him because of our ages and what we were going through. We were just being teenagers. I'm sorry that I didn't get to enjoy his life while he was alive.

I don't keep any pictures of my brother or my father around the house. I try not to think about it. But my mother is constantly thinking about my brother. She's constantly doing things that remind her of him. We have two very different ways of dealing with it. My mother will never, ever have closure. She lives and breathes my brother every single day.

On the twentieth anniversary of my brother's death, I was looking at the Facebook page my mother created about him. I came across this open letter that she wrote to him twelve years after he was murdered:

My Precious Joey, it's been twelve years. How can that be? In some ways it seems like a hundred years, but in others, just yesterday. How can everybody go on with their lives? I sometimes get upset that they can, because for me life stands still and I am stuck in time on the day you went away. There are days I seem to do better and then I feel guilty. How can I look forward to the future that doesn't have you in it. My heart is broken in tiny pieces and I can't put it back together. Nobody can but you. I know you are in a wonderful place where there is no pain, no tears, no sorrow.

But I'm human and a mom and the human mind is selfish. I want you with me to hug and to tell you how much I love you and hear your one-of-a-kind laugh again. Is there anything that I would have done different if I had known that this would be the last I would see

*you. I would have drove further and further
away. Never letting you go, keeping you safe
with me. I feel guilty because as your mom
I was supposed to keep you safe always. We
always let each other know how much we
loved each other. How deeply I loved you.
I thank God for 23 years we had. I cherish
every second and the memories of these
seconds fill my heart and mind each day.*

*What was your last thought, my son? I
pray that you didn't have time to think—not
knowing what was happening. That God
called your name and you went so quickly
from this earth to him. Joey, do you know how
much you are missed? Words can't describe
living in this world without you. Your last
words to me, you said, "I love you." Why
didn't I get a warning and just grab you and
take you far away? Sorry for the tears and
hurt, Joey. I know you hated it if I would cry
but I miss you. I buried a part of myself that
day with you. Hold on to that part, Joey, until
we meet again.*

If I had one more second with my brother, I would
tell him how beautiful his daughter is. I would tell
him that she has his eyes and it's like looking into his
eyes. I would tell him that he would be so proud of
her because she's come a long way in all these years.
She's almost twenty-five now. She's standing up for
herself and she wants to be part of her father's family.

If I had one more second with my brother, I would
tell him that I was sorry for taking for granted all the

days that he was here. I would tell him that I was sorry for all the times I could have hugged him or kissed him, but I didn't.

Sometimes he would grab me and pick me up, and I'd tell him to stop because he was so strong that he would squeeze the air out of me. Now I wish I hadn't told him to stop. I wish I had let him squeeze the air out of me or pick me up and swing me around. So what if I got dizzy?

All those things annoyed me when we were kids. I wish I could take back all those things I said about being annoyed. I wish I could tell him that I want him to tease me, make fun of me and annoy me.

I've felt so guilty about that, always. Even now, I feel guilty that I never got to spend that time with him. When you're a kid, you're going out, you're having a good time, and you're hanging out with your friends. You're not thinking that your brother is going to die when he's twenty-three years old. You're not thinking that, so you just take things for granted. You don't realize that this could happen. He could have just walked out the door and been hit by a car. But who thinks of that when you're a kid? You just don't think of it.

If I had one more second with my brother, I would tell him that I was sorry—so, so sorry I couldn't be there for him. Sorry that I couldn't help him. Sorry that he died that way. Sorry that I never got to show him how much I needed him. Sorry that I never told him how much I loved him. I did need him and I did love him. But I didn't show him enough.

I'm sorry.

NOTES AND SOURCES

Chapter 5

March 20, 1962, Memorandum to J. Edgar Hoover, Debriefing Gregory Scarpa Senior.

Fredric Dannen, "The G-Man and the Hit Man," *New Yorker,* December 16, 1996.

Anthony Villano, with Gerald Astor, *Brick Agent: Inside the Mafia for the FBI* (New York: Quadrangle, 1977), pp. 98–100.

David Stout, "Byron De La Beckwith Dies; Killer of Medgar Evers Was 80," *The New York Times,* January 3, 2001.

Judge W.O. "Chet" Dillard, *The Final Curtain: Burning Mississippi by the FBI* (Denver: Outskirts Press, 2007), pp. 71–75.

Shaila Dewan, "Former Klansman Guilty in 1964 Deaths," *The New York Times,* June 22, 2005.

"The FBI's Lin DeVecchio and 'The Grim Reaper,'" CBS, http://www.cbsnews.com/news/the-fbis-lin-devecchio-and-the-grim-reaper/ (May 22, 2011).

Captain Rodney Stich, *Crimes of the FBI-DOJ, Mafia and al Qaeda,* 2nd ed. (Alamo: Silverpeak Enterprises, 2010), p. 282.

Chapter 6

David M. Herszenhorn, "New Indictment for Reputed Colombo Crime Family Captain," *New York Times,* July 7, 1995.

Todd Venezia, "FBI Tied on Agent to Hit Mafia Beauty," *New York Post,* February 17, 2006.

Chapter 8

"Black Americans and HIV/AIDS," The Henry J. Kaiser Family Foundations, last modified April 25, 2014. http://kff.org/hivaids/fact-sheet/black-americans-and-hiv-aids.

Mary B.W. Tabor, "Settlement in Lawsuit on H.I.V.-Tainted Blood," *The New York Times,* August 30, 1992.

Todd S. Purdum, "Reputed Mob Figure Fatally Shot in Brooklyn Club," *The New York Times,* June 16, 1987.

Joseph Fried, "Howard Beach Defendant Given Maximum Term of 10 to 30 Years," *The New York Times,* January 23, 1988.

Arnold H. Lubasch, "Persico, His Son and 6 Others Get Long Terms as Colombo Gangsters," *The New York Times,* November 18, 1986.

Arnold H. Lubasch, "Prosecutors Tell of Colombo Family Murder Plot," *The New York Times,* September 1, 1991.

"Bad Blood," CBS, *Street Stories,* November 12, 1992.

Chapter 16

Jerry Capeci, "Capo's Son Gets 6 Yrs. In Plea Deal," *New York Daily News,* September 10,1999.

Jerry Capeci, "Get It in Writing," *Gang Land News,* September 23, 1999.

Jerry Capeci, *Jerry Capeci's Gang Land* (New York: Penguin, 2003), pp. 262–264.

Chapter 17

Kevin Gray, "The Mobster Who Brought Down the Mob," *Men's Journal,* October 2011.

Chapter 18

William K. Rashbaum, "Retired F.B.I. Agent Is Accused of Role in Killings," *The New York Times,* March 31, 2006.

Scott Shifrel, Joe Gould, Melissa Grace, "Judge in Lindley DeVecchio Case Rips FBI," *New York Daily News,* November 2, 2007.

Michael Brick, "At Trial of Ex-F.B.I. Supervisor, How to Love a Mobster," *The New York Times,* October 30, 2007.

Tom Robbins, "Tall Tales of a Mafia Mistress," *The Village Voice,* October 23, 2007.

Michael Brick, "Ex-F.B.I. Agent's Trial Fizzles, as Does Witness," *The New York Times,* November 1, 2007.

ACKNOWLEDGMENTS

To my children: You are my life, my everything, my reason for living. Without you, I don't know where I would be. You all have made my life complete. Mommy loves you for all the days of our lives. I will be forever thankful for you.

Mom, I never imagined that you could survive what you have survived. You have shown me strength and courage and I love you. Dad, you'll always be my hero. Linda Maria, always know I'm here for you. I love you so much. My nephew Gregory, you've come so far. Thank you for always showing me that you love me. Charlie, regardless of our circumstances, you will always have a place in my heart and I will always love you. Gavin, my little buddy, your smile will always be with me no matter how far apart we are.

Eddie Zorak, your strength inspires me. Thank you for showing me that it's possible to stay strong through traumatic experiences. Michael Holliman, from day one you have shown me nothing but support and friendship. You are greatly appreciated.

G Fella, I can't sing a song for you, but this is my way to thank you. Bud Light Bob, your light will always shine. I miss you. A special thank-you to my friends on Facebook for all the support and love you all have shown.

Billy Pietrantonio, you once said that you weren't afraid to die, you were afraid of not living. I want you to know that you'll live in my heart forever.

Michaela Hamilton, our editor at Kensington, thank you for believing in my story.

Linda Rosencrance, you never gave up on me. You believed in me when I didn't even believe in myself. I am so grateful to you for all you've done and helped me accomplish. You are an amazing person and will always have a special place in my heart. Thank you is not enough to express what I feel for you.—LS

I'd like to thank Michaela Hamilton at Kensington for being the best editor ever and for believing in this project. Plus a special shout-out to Ranger.

Lynn Riedesel, you are the best transcriptionist in the entire world. You are a lifesaver. Thank you.

Big Linda, your daughter is right. You are a strong and courageous person. I'm so glad I met you.

I was introduced to Linda Scarpa by a mutual friend several years ago. When I first heard her compelling story, I knew she had to share it with the world. She has lived a life that you could only imagine in your dreams—and your nightmares. Linda, to say that you are a survivor is an understatement. I am in awe of your courage. You are a remarkable mother, daughter, sister and friend. I never doubted your strength and determination—not for one second— even if you did. You can't imagine how very happy I am that you achieved your dream of seeing your words in print.

But it was more than about writing a book for you. It was about showing people who your father, your hero, truly was through your eyes. To do that, you had to be honest about the life that he led. The fact is, you were brutally honest about your life and his life. You didn't hide from the truth. And that took more courage than people will ever know.

As I grew closer to you over these past few years, I also felt a connection to your father. I came to understand through you that your father was not the monster people make him out to be. That's not to say I condone what he did, because I don't, and I know you don't, either. But he was a loving family man. Maybe in a different time and a different place . . . —LR

GREAT BOOKS,
GREAT SAVINGS!

When You Visit Our Website:
www.kensingtonbooks.com
You Can Save Money Off The Retail Price
Of Any Book You Purchase!

- **All Your Favorite Kensington Authors**
- **New Releases & Timeless Classics**
- **Overnight Shipping Available**
- **eBooks Available For Many Titles**
- **All Major Credit Cards Accepted**

Visit Us Today To Start Saving!
www.kensingtonbooks.com